Advance Praise

"Jayne Ellegard's book is a gem for women hoping to advance their financial lives. She has a unique ability to cut away the judgment and get right to work on the best strategies to refocus your goals. Through every step, she guides you with questions and actions meant to shore up information and start acting on a cohesive process. Whether you are looking for a few tips, or struggle in a shame spiral of debt, read this book.

Reading this book is like hanging out with a terrifically smart friend who knows the tricks and methods to help you create your financially abundant life. She has heard every story, from massive debt to faking money, so put the shame aside. Get the book, do the work, and watch your financial life transform."

Maureen Aitken, editor and award-winning author of *The Patron Saint of Lost Girls*.

"Jayne demystifies managing wealth by encouraging women to discuss money in a simple yet purposeful manner. Looking at the future ahead for my three daughters, I believe this book is a movement, empowering generations like my girls to be courageous and confident around topics of money. Backed by a solid expertise, Jayne is passionate and committed to helping women navigate the management of their wealth. This book is a great guide for most women (and for most men) who should be more confident when it comes to discussing their financial goals and aspirations."

Chady AlAhmar, CEO, Wealth Management, Old National Wealth Management

"*Financial Empowerment for Women* by Jayne Ellegard provides a set of exceptional tools to have in your financial knowledge toolbox. Her "pillar" approach creates the solid foundation upon which you can understand your financial capital. Taking her class helped me sit up straighter at investment meetings, be even more engaged in conversations around financial matters for my company and for me, and put my total legacy in clear perspective. I have retired with greater financial acumen due to my work with Ms. Ellegard."

Nancy JP Anderson, former owner of a privately held $100,000,000 company.

"The Girl Scout mission is to build girls of courage, confidence, and character, who make the world a better place. Jayne's mission is closely aligned with a focus on financial empowerment and the positive impact that can have on a woman's life and her legacy. This should be required reading for women of all ages!"

Tish Bolger, Chief Executive Officer, Girl Scouts River Valleys

"'A slinky low-cut number is more aggressive than a buttoned-up tailored shirt.' That's the difference between a portfolio with more stocks versus one with more bonds. Who in the hell talks about investments like that? Jayne Ellegard, that's who! And that is PRECISELY why you are going to devour her book the way I just did. By page 3, I was already shouting out loud 'Where have you been all my life?' Her stories are inspiring, but even more remarkable … for the first time in my life, I finally understand (and I mean REALLY understand) how to make, save and grow my own money. WOW. She offers simple and fun analogies (read above) that just make it all so clear. And then she serves up smart, bite-sized solutions that EVERY woman (regardless of age, income or upbringing) can understand and use. It's a remarkable read.

I've been battling financial demons my entire life. Terrible lessons from my mother. Terrifying lessons from my dad. Despite all that, I saved and spent wisely. So why … when I started making good money and getting the life I dreamed of, was I riddled with guilt and shame about my financial success. Turns out, I am not alone! This book is the gift EVERY daughter should receive as she steps out into the world. And then, she should read it again every single year. Jayne's stories are inspiring and relatable, but it's her 30+ years of rock-solid financial industry expertise that makes her book so valuable. Laugh along with it. Do the simple, bite-sized solutions she recommends.

Then sit back and feel the calm and eventually joy start to fill your life. Financial security IS within your reach … but you've got to stand up and go get it."

Cat Breet, Chief Stripe Changer, ARBEZ

"Growing up, money was only for a selected few. It made people do all kinds of silly things. And almost always, it was a source of tears. In 2021, so many of us are still holding onto limiting beliefs around money. But what if we could completely redefine money? What if we could make it our friend and a source of joy? That is precisely what is at the heart of this book for me. Jayne has spent decades helping women move from shame and confusion to feeling empowered and confident about money. She does that now for all of us in this masterful blend of gentle encouragement and practical steps that we can all follow."

Jasna Burza, Life and Business Strategist, JBC

"I wish Jayne Ellegard's book was gifted to me as a young professional. Jayne does an excellent job at encouraging the reader to cultivate a healthy and positive relationship with money. Jayne utilizes the power of storytelling to connect with her readers in an authentic, transparent, and down-to-earth manner. This book is both informative and transformational."

Dr. Jermaine M. Davis, Award-winning Professor of Communication & Leadership, Author of *Leading with Greatness*

"Jayne offers a unique mix of expertise, inspiration and compassion that will motivate you to get engaged in your financial journey! She has written this book with the reader in mind, explaining how to translate best practices into your daily life and how to confidently empower yourself to take control of your financial future. She is authentic and passionate in her mission to move women forward in a powerful way and she provides ample examples to "bring to life" some of the best principles for financial leadership. *Financial Empowerment for Women* provides a refreshing approach to understanding the role money plays in your life. Readers will benefit from her special gift for communicating the essential concepts women need to know when making financial decisions."

Richard K. Davis, President & CEO, Make-A-Wish America

"Financial Empowerment for Women is GREAT for many reasons…from a man's perspective. Jayne is a patient, *Ellegant* teacher and guide – much better than I am on both counts. Jayne's approach is wonderful for all women (and men too) - she has been successful with my wife, daughter, sister-in-law, mother-in-law (and me), which covers a variety of ages, educational levels and financial status. Jayne truly helps women who have been born with money (wealth), earned their money, inherited money while previously having struggled financially and everyone in between!"

Dave Dovenberg, former Chairman of Universal Hospital Services

"In *Financial Empowerment for Women,* Jayne Ellegard brings the reader through a logical and confidence building process with her Six Pillars. In each section she finds a way to connect the financial concepts to things women will relate to, bringing a deeper understanding. This book is needed to help women in their financial literacy journey."

Heather Ettinger, CEO and Founder, Luma Wealth, best-selling author, Lumination: Shining a Light on a Woman's Journey to Financial Wellness

"Financial Empowerment for Women is written by a highly successful financial professional, Jayne Ellegard, who chose to leave her career and create a program to bring this, financial empowerment, to women. Jayne's book takes us though the Six Pillars of Financial Empowerment in an easy and fun way using illustrations from her own life (and others) with honesty, sensitivity and humor. Why commit the time for this book in an already overloaded life? Often there comes a time when women HAVE TO learn about finances because of a death or a divorce. What a terrible time to learn something new; when you and those around you are all grieving. Be prepared for your future and have some fun along the way. **Grab your book club** and walk through the exercises together."

Jacqueline (Jacie) Fogelberg, MBA, SVP Wealth Advisor, Old National Wealth Management

"This book is like having a good friend talk to me about my relationship with money without judgement. Jayne opens the conversation of the real role money plays as a wife, mother, friend, professional, community member. I saw myself and the women I care about in the stories throughout. Jayne takes complex financial concepts and makes them easy to understand without being condescending. The pillars in this book are actionable and so empowering. Saving, spending, investing, planning, enjoying, this book is a must have for women at any age, the younger the better.

As a result of the exploratory and consultative tone of this book, I uncovered some of the troublesome messages I had told myself. When my parents divorced in the 80s my mom was devastated that she couldn't get a credit card. Nearly 40 years later I confronted how those feelings of fear and uncertainty defined my own relationship with money and I have been encouraged to assuage feelings of guilt or shame and to consider what I want to nurture for my future, and I have a plan to do so."

Robin Kellogg, Speaker • Workplace Facilitator, RobinKellogg.com

"WOW! I just read this book! What a fascinating read! We, as women, have to know about money and as we get older it is more and more important! I have seen so many of my friends over the years get in trouble because they did not understand their money situation! Jayne's book helps us all grasp the importance of knowing about our money. This book should have been written years ago but, at least, we have it now. I can't wait to give it to my daughter."

Jean Ketcham, Founder, Aging But DANGEROUS.COM®

"When solving problems, mathematicians, engineers, and others often use the term 'elegant solution', referencing the maximum best outcome achievable with the smallest or simplest effort. Jayne Ellegard's *Financial Empowerment for Women* is any woman's elegant solution for taking care of herself financially. The book is filled with interesting facts, anecdotes and case studies, with worksheets, and is conveniently organized into six useful 'Pillars' of financial knowledge. I enjoyed this book, and learned from it, seeing myself in her stories."

Gailen Krug, retired Chief Investment Officer, retired alternative asset consultant, and current Family Office Trustee and Board member.

"Jayne has written the blueprint and manifesto for getting your financial house in order. She shares what you need to know and do in order to build a foundation for your financial wellness and future. Keep her book within arms' reach and refer to it often. You will be glad you did and will never be the same – only better for it! Your bank account will be better too."

Mark LeBlanc, CSP, Author of *Never Be The Same* and *Growing Your Business!*

"Jayne has a wonderful knack for telling stories that make conversations about money interesting and relatable. She addresses the emotions and stereotypes head on, creating a practical and engaging guide for women to address their financial well-being."

Michele L. Martin, President, Lurie Wealth Advisors

"Jayne has choreographed a perfect balance of financial education with contextual relevance, helping readers better connect their money with the purpose of their wealth. All of this is designed to build financial empowerment no matter where you are in your life: whether you are just getting started, in your peak wealth building years or navigating a life transition such as divorce or widowhood. Jayne's book is a fresh and timely guide that will surely help many women take charge of their finances with clarity and confidence."

Angie O'Leary, Head, Wealth Planning, RBC Wealth Management

"Throughout my career I have met countless people who feel that aspects of personal wealth management are too complex and intimidating to address. Jayne demonstrates that the concepts are largely common sense, very understandable and actionable. *Financial Empowerment for Women* strips away the confusing jargon and translates it to understandable concepts for anyone new to these matters. Jayne's approach starts with the basics and builds the foundation for you to be empowered and take control of your situation, from the earliest steps to a full understanding of the big picture. In the end, Jayne walks you through the process to answer the most important questions you can ask yourself, 'What do I want and how do I accomplish it?'"

John Pohlad, Chief Revenue Officer, Marquette Wealth Management

"Jayne's book provides the thoughtful, insightful, and practical methodology to close the financial education gap for women. The 6 pillars provide a framework, tools, and resources to support you in understanding your financial situation. Applying these lessons, and taking action, no matter where you are starting from, you will develop a deeper awareness of what makes you tick with money. As you develop your own action plans and habits, you will experience a feeling of confidence, control, and self-assuredness with money conversations and money decisions. And as the book title says, you will have the courage, confidence, and wisdom to become a financially empowered woman!"

Mary Schmid, MBA, Author of *Make or Break Conversations: How Smart Financial Professionals Land New Clients and Keep Them for Life*

"Even more profound than her deep expertise in women and finance, is her ability to see, understand, and connect with her client's experience. She has the unique gift of illuminating the story, meaning, and impact behind numbers, and transforming what is often a stressful process into one that is empowering. Only Jayne could write a book that helps women truly get to the heart of the matter and step into their full financial potential."

Katie Spencer, Founder, Northbound Consulting

"Money is not the answer to all your problems, but money provides options to solve most problems. *Financial Empowerment for Women: Your Guide to Courage, Confidence, and Wisdom!* is a must-read for women desiring to become comfortable understanding and managing how to make their money work for them. If you're seeking financial peace this is the book for you."

Jasmine Brett Stringer, Speaker and Award-Winning Author of Seize Your Life: How to Carpe Diem Every Day

"Jayne erases embarrassment by building financial confidence and courage. Using relatable examples, straightforward descriptions and useful activities, this book informs and empowers. Jayne walks us not only through gaining an understanding of our money obstacles and personalities but also equips us to move beyond our limiting beliefs and circumstances. This is a great book for anyone ready to take action on being leaders vs followers with their finances."

Teresa Thomas, Win Win Connects, author and expert on connection and joy

"Jayne creates the perfect process for women to learn about money (and their relationship with it) in a non-threatening, fun-loving way. She provides just the right amount of teaching through breaking concepts into steps and providing an opportunity for building greater self-awareness through introspection. She is uniquely wired to be able to do both beautifully and elegantly (or should I say ellegantly)."

Ruth Tongen, President, Ivy Consulting

"Finally, a tangible, relevant and kind way to learn about all things financial! Financial Empowerment for Women is a must read, especially for the woman who has lost touch with your financial life. Personally, I've done just that, lost touch and grew complacent. Jayne's book lit a fire within to actively do research, set goals, voice more ideas and angles for investing our money while reconnecting fully to the reigns on our financial life. It's made quite a difference! Thank you, Jayne, you brought my power back into my financial life!"

Amy Vasterling, Founder of the Wisdom Gathering

Financial Empowerment for Women

Selene,
Be financially
inspired!

Financial Empowerment for Women

Your Guide to Courage, Confidence & Wisdom!

Jayne Ellegard

Printed in the United States of America
First printing, March 2021

First edition

ISBN: 978-1-946195-88-3
Library of Congress Control Number: 2021900208

Photo Credits: Lori Knisely (back cover); UG Production (About the Author and Speaking Engagements)
Images created by Textile Creative Studios
Cover Design & Interior Book Design: Ann Aubitz

Published by FuzionPress
1250 E 115th Street, Burnsville, MN 55337
612-781-2815

To order, visit www.ellegantwealth.com
Quantity discounts available.

Dedication

To my mom—you have been an amazing role model in my life, paving the way as a working mother, exercising on your lunch hour, publishing the first of three books at the age of sixty-five and the most recent at eighty-four. You've shown me that anything is possible, and I'm proud to follow in your footsteps!

To every woman who makes the decision to transform her financial life!

Foreword

Research tells us that women would rather talk about their own death than money. Jayne Ellegard is on a heartfelt mission to change that and put women confidently in charge of their own finances. Jayne and I have been colleagues for over 20 years and continue to reunite on the topic of women and their wealth. Jayne has deep expertise in the financial services industry as an accomplished advisor, portfolio manager, speaker, and financial coach. I was thrilled to hear about Jayne's impressive endeavor to bring that expertise to life in her new book *Financial Empowerment for Women.*

By all measures, women have reached new heights in education, earnings, and economic power. Women in the United States now control the majority of the wealth, and many of them will control their family wealth at some point in their lives. Yet, there's ambivalence about the role women should play in their personal finances. This confidence gap extends beyond financial literacy and requires a fresh approach to building financial skills that empower women.

While there are numerous books in this category, Jayne's book rises to the top for many reasons. Most importantly, it provides the reader with a credible and comprehensive guide to finances—and does so with a feminine flair that is highly engaging. The book is also hands on, with actionable steps that help readers track their progress. And it's chock-full of first-hand wisdom from other women who are making a similar journey.

Jayne has choreographed a perfect balance of financial education with contextual relevance, helping readers better connect their money with the purpose of their wealth. All of this is designed to build financial empowerment no matter where you are in life: whether you are just getting started, in your peak wealth-building years, or navigating a life transition such as divorce or widowhood. Jayne's book is a fresh and timely guide that will surely help many women take charge of their finances with clarity and confidence.

Angie O'Leary, Head, Wealth Planning, RBC Wealth Management

Table of Contents

Notes

People often look at the name of my company, Ellegant Wealth, and wonder why Ellegant is spelled with two l's. It is a play on my last name—Ellegard, but there is also a fun double meaning: "Elle" is French for she, and my company focuses on financial education for women. It seemed like the perfect name. But I do know how to spell, in case you were wondering. 😊

Throughout this book, I have included stories from women whose identities are kept confidential. I am grateful to each of them for their permission to share their beautiful thoughts and insights. Some are women who have participated in a group coaching or online course I've taught; others are friends who have disclosed their stories. I have paraphrased certain comments to protect confidentiality. My hope is you will see yourself in one or more of them and know that transformation is also possible for you.

Introduction

"She believed she could, so she did."
—Unknown

Ellegant Introduction

Do you struggle with money? Maybe feel confused by it at times? If you have, I can assure you, you're not alone. I hear many women say they find it frustrating, intimidating, and boring.

Jill, an attorney, said, "My knowledge about money is low. I don't speak the speak. It's all Greek to me, so I disengage. But I can and should understand it. I know I NEED to understand it. This doesn't fit the image I have of myself as a smart, professional woman." Can you relate to how Jill feels?

Carol is a musician. She had no access to financial education while she was in school, and when she married her husband, he was only too happy to manage the finances for both of them. Before he passed away, he wisely asked their daughter, who had a financial background, to take over. Carol grew uncomfortable with dumping her total financial responsibility on her daughters' shoulders. She started looking around for a personal finance class and found mine.

After completing the course, Carol said, "What strikes me is that you helped me understand my role and responsibility in managing my wealth. You opened a door that I had tried to nail shut, by showing me that despite my antipathy, finance IS a big part of my life. I can shut my eyes and let others lead me, or I can open them and decide what I want and where I want to go. I now have the confidence *and enthusiasm* to explore this whole new world that has been opened up to me."

I want all of that for you. I want you to want all of that for you.

According to the study by UBS entitled "Own Your Worth 2020,"[1] 49% of women in the United States defer long-term financial decisions to their spouse or partner. When asked why, they identified a host of reasons, most of which fell into four broad categories: lack of confidence, complacency, entrenched roles, and a desire to keep the peace in their relationships. Overall, most women who defer tend to believe their spouses know more about investing and other long-term decisions.

It's time to get fearless about finances and take control of your financial journey!

This book is for you if you can relate to any of the following statements:

1. I want financial security.
2. I'm stressed about money.
3. I love spending money.
4. I feel guilty when I spend money.
5. I have a lot of money.
6. I have no money.
7. I don't like talking about money.
8. I wish I knew more about money.
9. I'm not good with numbers.
10. I don't want to ask stupid questions.
11. I'm afraid of money.
12. I have a complicated financial situation.
13. I have shame around money.
14. I'm overwhelmed by money.
15. I don't know where to start.

---

[1] UBS. "Own Your Worth 2020," (2020): 8, https://advisors.ubs.com/fwmgsara-sota/mediahandler/media/323256/own-your-worth-report-2020.pdf

16. I don't trust anyone in the financial industry.
17. I don't like taking any risks with my money.
18. I don't want to invest and then lose money.
19. I'm not worthy.

The list could continue for pages.

Bottom line: this book is meant to provide
every woman who reads it with a simple,
easy to understand approach to understanding her financial situation.

Whether your situation is

- very simple or incredibly complex,
- you've been recently divorced or widowed, and your husband handled the finances,
- you're the breadwinner but hate numbers,
- you make good money, but somehow the debt keeps piling up, or
- you've just lost your job and can't breathe,

you will benefit from the process this book will provide.

Bottom line: this book is meant to provide every woman who reads it with a simple, easy to understand approach to understanding her financial situation.

I've found there is so much shame around money. It doesn't seem to matter if you have no money, a lot of money, or you're somewhere in between. Maybe you're hanging onto every bad money decision you've ever made, don't feel you deserve the money you have accumulated, or you're beating yourself up for not saving enough.

> The reality is your financial situation is never going away—EVER! It's going to be there. Every. Single. Day.

Have you ever heard anyone say one of their top values is money? It would be like admitting you're greedy. Yet, how many people are truly driven and motivated by money? It provides many wonderful things—among them freedom, flexibility, security, and the ability to truly make a difference in the world (if you choose to do that with your money).

But for some reason, there's embarrassment. What is it about money that makes us so uncomfortable? It doesn't matter who you are. I've seen really smart, confident women have absolutely no grasp of the concept. I've seen them in tears, overwhelmed and scared.

The reality is your financial situation is never going away—EVER! It's going to be there. Every. Single. Day. It's pretty hard to escape, although we can make a pretty good attempt by binge-watching our favorite Netflix show or getting sucked into our best friend's drama.

Rather than try to avoid it, we're going to face it—head on—TOGETHER. I'll be with you every step of the way. I know you. I've worked with someone like you. I know how you got here and what's holding you back. I can help you. I will help you. If you let me.

It's time for us to change the narrative about becoming financially successful women. Would you rather be the damsel in distress or someone who is self-assured and confident in their money decisions? Men and women have been in an imbalance for so long. Women have minimized themselves at times, so they don't stand out. We need to level up and claim our seats at the table as equals.

Money is one of the essential building blocks to overall wellness. There is often so much focus on nutrition, exercise, mindfulness, and so on, but the financial aspect seems to get lost somewhere along the way. Gaining financial security for yourself frees you up to do so much more for others. It allows you to have a significant impact in areas that are meaningful to you.

There is a gap in the financial education women have received. It's not your fault. Nobody taught you this. Women often enjoy learning collaboratively. It's why we have book clubs and come up with other reasons to gather. But what's the one thing we aren't talking about? Money. In my experience, money is still treated as a taboo subject by many people. If we open up and start talking about it, we can learn from one another. If you have a circle of friends you *are* discussing it with, that's fantastic! I applaud you for breaking down the barrier. Unfortunately, that's rare.

This is my passion! I thoroughly enjoyed what I did before, helping my clients achieve their financial goals. I loved earning their trust and building meaningful relationships with them. But this is what I feel I was meant to do, where it was all leading. The pull toward coaching and making a difference in people's lives was strong. I saw too many women thrown into scary situations due to the death

Money is one of the essential building blocks to overall wellness.

of a spouse or an unexpected divorce and decided I needed to do something to make a difference. My goal is to encourage as many women as possible to be proactive and get in front of the significant life events that can occur. Join me now wherever you are in your unique financial journey.

Let's get started!

"They say it is better to be poor and happy than rich and miserable, but how about a compromise like moderately rich and just moody?"
—Princess Diana, Princess of Wales

Ellegant Welcome

Before we jump in, I'd like you to think about why you purchased this book. What are you hoping to gain at the end of our journey together?

I've asked other women to share what they wanted to achieve by learning more about their finances. Here is a sampling of things they've said:

- Financial alignment and partnership with my spouse or family
- Better conversations around money with my family and friends
- Peace and contentment around money
- Reduced financial stress
- Feeling "smart" about money

- Feeling confident in my financial situation
- Knowing I'm well-served by my Advisors
- Instilling financial competence in my children and grand-children
- Overcome a deeply held belief that I'm not good with numbers
- Asking not just smart questions, but the right questions

But what is YOUR reason? Why are you here?
Write your thoughts below:

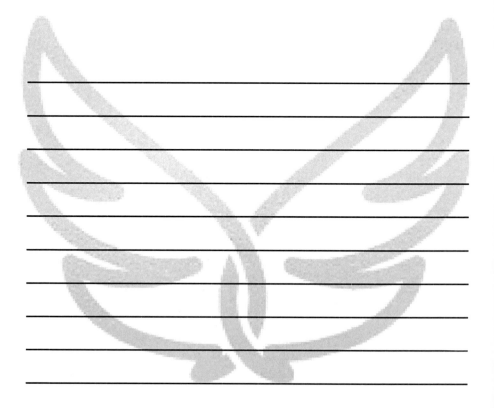

Something that I often get asked is, "When should I start doing all of this? When should I start thinking about my financial situation? Am I too late? Is it too early?"

First, it's never too late. Second, it's never too early. Start now. Right now!

I get it. It can be hard if you're in your fifties, sixties, or seventies, and you don't have enough money saved for retirement. But beating yourself up for what you wish you had done differently isn't going to change anything in the past. All you can do is start learning and modifying your behaviors today.

First, it's never too late. Second, it's never too early. Start now. Right now!

Linda, who is in her late sixties, shared this:

> *I was a reluctant member of one of Jayne's groups at first. I thought since I was beyond retirement age, my financial future was fixed, the decisions made in the past were set in stone, and there was no way to recover. She listened to my concerns and recommended that I just might find something of value. She was right. I learned that being absent in my decisions about my finances and handing them off to those I trusted didn't absolve me of my responsibility. While they may have been making good decisions for me, I needed to know what was happening rather than glazing over. Now I have a much better understanding of those concepts and my values and how I can make a difference to my future. One is never too old to learn something new, embrace change and lay a better foundation for the future.*

If you're young, you have the opportunity to make a significant difference in your life by getting on top of this sooner rather than later. Don't push it off and wait for "the right time." Get good financial habits in place and stick with them. You'll be glad you did!

June, who is in her mid-thirties, shared this:

Money can be an easy topic to avoid, and it can be overwhelming and intimidating. My fear has been replaced with confidence. I expected to learn about investments and understand my financial situation, but what I didn't expect was to have a greater belief in myself. For the first time in twelve years, I raised the prices in my business because I know I'm worth it! I provide an incredible service for my clients, and I deserve to be compensated appropriately. Most of my clients said it was about time. I'm glad I figured this out now, but wish I would have learned it years ago.

"If you think taking care of yourself is selfish, change your mind."
—Ann Richards, the 45th governor of Texas

Ellegant Wealth Mission Statement: Empowering women to "show up" and own their financial journey with Courage, Confidence, & Wisdom!

My senior year in college, I went home for Christmas. The first night, my mom and dad took me out to dinner at the Spot Supper Club to celebrate my being home for the holidays. During dinner, the conversation turned to graduation. My dad made it very clear that he thought I should have a job lined up. He said, "The day you graduate, you're done. I'm not giving you another dollar. You better figure it out."

My dad definitely believed in the tough love approach. When my brother and sister (older and far more athletic than me) were little, he would take them out in the boat to the middle of the lake, throw them in, and let them swim back to shore. He didn't do that to me because I'm pretty sure he knew I'd drown. But here it was, coming back to haunt me in a slightly different way. I ran from the table in tears.

I had some pretty big student loans and no money saved. I was a poor college student. Fortunately, I managed to get a job offer right before I graduated. I mean *days* before I graduated. I moved in with my brother and his family for a couple of months so I could get a little money tucked away. Then, I rented a room in a house with two other girls I didn't know. I had a mattress on the floor and very few belongings.

It honestly didn't even occur to me to rack up debt on a credit card. I'm not sure why. Maybe it was that good Midwest upbringing. I just learned to live within my means. Nobody was going to help me, so I had to figure it out for myself. So I did. I knew I didn't want to live that frugally forever.

Don't get me wrong, my parents loved me. My mom would buy me groceries and supplies when I went home. My dad would give me gas money. They lived six hours away from where I was living. Looking back, it was the best thing they could have done for me. Moving back to the small town I grew up in and living with my parents wasn't a choice. Succeeding was the only option.

Courage, Confidence, & Wisdom

I'm so excited for you to transform your financial life! Reading this book will help you get your arms firmly wrapped around your financial situation. You will no longer be a deer in headlights, you won't have your head buried in the sand, your eyes won't glaze over in the meetings with your financial advisor or planner, and you won't be wondering why your advisor is speaking a foreign language.

You will be empowered to show up and own your financial journey with courage, confidence, and wisdom! By spending the time investing in yourself, you are going to have the following attributes:

1. **Courage** to be Proactive!
   - Life events happen. They can be scary and overwhelming. If you can get in front of these events, you will provide yourself with peace of mind. Start learning now.

2. **Confidence** to Own Your Financial Power!
   - The conversations happening today about your financial situation impact you now and in the future. Don't let someone else (advisor, partner, father) make these significant decisions for you. Get involved in the discussion.
3. **Wisdom** to Be the Hero—or the Shero! (I love that term.)
   - If you don't understand your financial situation, you probably also aren't having conversations about money that you could and should be having with your parents, children, or partner. By learning more, you can start to share your knowledge with the people you love. So, if you feel guilty about spending this time on yourself, do it for your family. You will all benefit!

After a weekend workshop I held in a small community in the state of Wyoming, I said to Deb as she was leaving, "I hope you feel financially empowered!" She turned to me and said, "Jayne, I don't think you understand the impact you've had here. You've not just empowered me. You've empowered my family and this entire community."

Never underestimate the power of learning, as well as sharing your knowledge with others. If you apply even some of the ideas shared with you here, you will experience a significant change in your financial life.

The three statements above answer the "why" question that might be rolling around in your head. What is your purpose, your cause, your belief? Why should I do this? Why is it important? Why should I care? The three topics we're going to cover—courage, confidence, and wisdom—are why I hope you're reading this book. It's why I wrote it!

Is it important for you to have courage, confidence, and wisdom when it comes to your financial journey? Let me provide you with some facts from the UBS, "Own Your Worth 2018"[2] report.

1. *Eight out of ten women end up on this journey alone.* This applies to those who never marry, are divorced, or are widowed. Now, I'm not

---

[2] UBS. "Own Your Worth 2018" (2018): Preface – 1, https://www.ubs.com/content/dam/WealthManagementAmericas/documents/2018-37666-UBS-Own-Your-Worth-report-R32.pdf

saying this is necessarily a bad thing. The alternative for the other two women isn't great—they avoid this predicament by dying first.

2. *Fifty-one percent of marriages end in divorce with gray divorce on the rise.* Gray divorce is a new term that has been coined because divorce among elderly couples has increased so dramatically.

3. Are you under the age of sixty? *The average age of widowhood in the United States is fifty-nine.* Let me repeat that. *The average age of widowhood in the United States is fifty-nine.* You do the math. Fifty is the new thirty. Imagine being a widow at the age of fifty-nine (or younger).

4. *Women outlive their husbands on average five years.* That's the average. If you are one of the women who experiences widowhood at a younger age, it could be significantly longer.

I'm telling you this because there is a very high likelihood you will need to step up and take responsibility for your financial situation at some point in time. I've worked with women who have experienced the sudden loss of a spouse or an unexpected divorce, and it was overwhelming. I don't want this to happen to you.

You might be thinking, *Is she trying to scare me?* You can be scared, *or* you can be inspired. Whatever you choose, I simply urge you to take action.

I know you DESERVE to be financially empowered. I know you NEED to be financially empowered. Be scared or be inspired, but get fearless about your finances NOW! I don't ever want you to struggle or feel confused about money again! I want you to be in control. Isn't that what you would want for your friends, your mother, your daughter? Why wouldn't you want that for yourself?

> You can be scared, *or* you can be inspired. Whatever you choose, I simply urge you to take action.

As we have so often been advised by flight attendants on every flight, "You must first put on your own oxygen mask before helping anyone else."

The same is true regarding your finances. You need to understand your own situation, your feelings around money, and the financial concepts before you can help the people you love. That's what we're here to accomplish.

I want this experience to be empowering and educational. I believe there is a gap in the education women are receiving around wealth. I intend to impact how you view your financial situation. I expect you to gain courage, confidence, and wisdom during our time together.

Many women have expressed to me their desire to communicate better with their spouse around this topic. My friend Donna said, "My husband drags me to those meetings with our advisor and then gets mad when I don't understand anything. I'm like a deer in headlights. I asked him one day if we have enough money saved to put our kids through college. He said, 'I give you the college fund statements every month.' I said, 'I know and I promptly shred them.' Obviously, I need to understand this better."

A Tale of Two Women

I want to introduce you to two women—very similar, smart, professional women with busy lives.

Meet Mary. Mary is a pediatrician who works part-time, so she can be more involved in her children's lives. She likes to cook and run marathons and prefers almost anything over investments. She has delegated the responsibility of the family finances to her husband, Mark. She makes every effort to attend as few of the meetings with their advisor as possible.

I wish I would have been more engaged when Mark was alive.

When we check in a few years later, Mary has blissfully continued to rely on Mark and their advisor to handle the finances. And then, Mark dies suddenly of a heart attack. Mary's world is turned upside down. Not only is she grieving, but she doesn't understand anything about their financial situation. Mary shared, "I'm scared. I don't know what this means financially to my children, my lifestyle, my retirement. I don't even really know if I can still afford to stay in my house.

It's overwhelming. I know my advisor will help me, but I realize I'm completely reliant on someone else. I wish I would have been more engaged when Mark was alive."

If any of you have lost your spouse, you feel Mary's pain. And my heart goes out to you. Or, maybe you have a friend who has had something similar happen to them. The advice most widows would give their friends is to get in front of it, to be proactive and get your arms around your financial situation before something happens. However, women often find it difficult to spend time and money on themselves. They wait for the trigger to happen and then wish they would have made the upfront investment.

Now, meet Sally. Sally is a partner with a small advertising firm and is very creative. She admits she hates math and is one of those women whose husband drags her to the meetings with the advisor and her eyes glaze over, thinking about all the other things she'd rather be doing.

I sat up straight and asked questions with confidence!

When we check in a few months later, Sally and her husband, Steve, recently met with their advisor. Sally shared the experience. "I sat up straight and asked questions with confidence! If I didn't understand what he was saying, I stopped him and asked him to explain the concept. It was by far the best meeting we've ever had with him. When we got home, Steve turned to me and said, 'I finally feel like we are financial partners. The financial burden is no longer entirely on my shoulders.' I had no idea he even felt that way."

Wow—what changed? Sally recognized that she needed to learn more about money and decided to join an Ellegance for Women group. Her husband, Steve, was encouraging and supportive. During the process, she worked through the Six Pillars to Financial Empowerment. Sally is thrilled she spent the time getting educated. She knows she still has a lot to learn but has clearly moved from the back seat to the front seat of her financial journey.

HAVE THE COURAGE TO BE PROACTIVE!

Don't wait to be thrown into a scary and overwhelming situation. Give yourself peace of mind knowing that you are as prepared as you can be when a life event occurs. Because life events will happen. It could be any number of things: the death of a spouse, divorce, a career change, an inheritance—a pandemic. You obviously know you need to start learning more about your financial situation, or you wouldn't be reading this book. It's one of those things that you recognize as important, but it never makes it to the top of the list. It's so easy to push it to the side, let it slide to the bottom of the pile, or promise yourself you'll get to it soon. But soon never really comes.

It's one of those things that you recognize as important, but it never makes it to the top of the list.

Examples of other activities that fall into the same category are exercising, meditating, writing in a gratitude journal, having a date night, and engaging in long-term planning. These are things that can have a wonderfully positive impact on your life. Are you carving out the time to make those happen? Most of us find time to watch our favorite show, scroll through social media, and order a cute pair of jeans online. But do any of those things really add tremendous value to your life? If you break down your personal wealth management into smaller time slots, like an hour to update your net worth statement or review last month's expenses, it won't feel quite as overwhelming.

Ignoring your finances is like having a teenager in the house and not paying any attention to them. A lot of damage can be done while you're mesmerized by *The Great British Baking Show*.

I am so proud of you for taking this huge step forward. You're ahead of the game already!

OUR Journey TOGETHER

"A woman's best protection is a little money of her own."
— Clare Boothe Luce, American author

Our Journey Together

This program is built on the Six Pillars to Financial Empowerment that I believe are the foundation for fully embracing your financial situation.

As each pillar is introduced, there will be stories from women who have taken one of my financial education programs and have shared an aspect of their financial journey—from before, during, or after their participation. I've also taken some stories from my own personal journey that I hope you will find valuable. I want you to find inspiration from these stories and possibly identify with one or more of these women. You are not alone in this journey, and everyone who has been in a similar situation wants to see you find your path to success.

You are not alone in this journey, and everyone who has been in a similar situation wants to see you find your path to success.

Even though you may have a thorough understanding of whatever subject is being covered, I would encourage you to read through all six pillars and listen to the stories being told. Spend time thinking about your own story around this topic. Consider others in your life—parents, spouse, children, grandchildren, friends, and hey, maybe even your book club. Use these stories to gain awareness around the concerns they might have. How can you learn from what others experienced and carry those conversations forward with those you love?

We all come to this space at different levels of knowledge or wealth and stages of life. When I bring women together as a group, I ask them to agree to some guidelines. I would like to ask you to consider some of these as well. Participate with an open heart. Come to this journey with a willingness to be honest with yourself. I hope you will offer yourself the space to allow for insights and the chance to discover yourself. Give yourself permission and take the time to assess your situation. Write down your thoughts in the space provided or start a separate journal to take notes.

Don't rush through this book. Consider reading a pillar a week. The pillars build on one another. I placed them in a very specific order. Work through the exercises and deeply consider the questions being asked. I know that can be hard. It is for me anyway. I want to rush through to the end and arrive at the answer. In this case, the answer is within you. You're going to need to think about your personal situation and pull together all the different pieces of information that make up the details of your circumstances. You may want to reread a chapter once you've gathered the suggested items or before (or after) a meeting with your advisor. Take your time and let it sink in, especially if this is your first time truly making a concerted effort in this space.

Money is one of the top reasons couples fight.

I would encourage you to take some of the questions being asked throughout this book and after thinking about your own responses, ask a loved one about their thoughts. This can spark healthy money discussions. Gaining a stronger understanding of why loved ones do what they do around money can provide amazing insights into your relationship. Money is one of the top reasons couples fight. It can cause a tremendous amount of friction, so while in a calm state of mind, have a conversation.

There is a funny YouTube video titled "Men's Brains vs. Women's Brains" or "Tale of Two Brains" with Mark Gungor of Laugh Your Way: A Couples' Comedy Event.[3] Google it and take the time to watch. It reinforces how we're different. In it, Mr. Gungor shares that women remember things. In particular, we remember events that have an emotion attached to them. (I know that's true for me.) For women, he says that everything is attached to everything. Men, on the other hand, prefer to keep things separated and have their favorite "nothing box."

It's an entertaining reminder that people process things differently, and it's valuable to consider how we want to communicate with each other when it comes to certain topics—especially money.

---

[3] "Men's Brains vs Women's Brains," YouTube video, 5:10, "wrksnfx," April 20, 2014, https://www.youtube.com/watch?v=0KrOZe2SxoQ&t=10s.

ELLEGANT
WEALTH

SIX PILLARS TO FINANCIAL EMPOWERMENT

1 EXPLORE YOUR MONEY BELIEFS	2 ESTABLISH YOUR FINANCIAL GOALS	3 KNOW YOUR NET WORTH
"Marry a Rich Man"	What's Your Destination?	Financial Starting Point

4 SPEND WITH PURPOSE	5 LEARN TO SPEAK "INVESTMENTS"	6 PROTECT AND PLAN
Treasures, Promises & Joy	The Perfect Outfit	Giving the Best Gifts

Six Pillars to Financial Empowerment

Meet the Six Pillars to Financial Empowerment!

Pillar 1: Explore Your Money Beliefs
What you heard about money growing up could be impacting the decisions you're making today. Let's uncover your money mindset.

Pillar 2: Establish Your Financial Goals
We all want something different for our future. Let's explore your dreams and goals.

Pillar 3: Know Your Net Worth
Gaining an awareness of your financial starting point, your net worth, is a valuable tool to help you move forward. Let's gain awareness around these numbers.

Pillar 4: Spend with Purpose
Spending money can be fun, but it can also lead to problems. Let's view spending from a slightly different perspective.

Pillar 5: Learn to Speak "Investments"

Investing can sound like a foreign language if you don't understand the lingo and the jargon. Let's unpack the meaning behind investments.

Pillar 6: Plan and Protect

Insurance and estate planning are important components of your overall financial situation. Let's uncover the value of wealth protection.

All of the pillars wrapped together allow us to design our heartfelt legacy—today and tomorrow.

Your financial situation is like a puzzle, and your puzzle is going to be different from everybody else's. You want to be certain you've gathered all the pieces, and they're all fitting together nicely to create a beautiful scenario.

What does your future look like?

What's the most important part of a puzzle? The picture on the box. I believe these six pillars are the key to helping you gain clarity and create the vision (or the picture on the box) of your financial puzzle. Maybe you chose the Italian Alps puzzle because you dream of going there someday or you chose the happy puppies puzzle because you love your dog. Having that vision will allow you to make clear financial choices that move you forward in a powerful way.

What does your future look like? What are the important pieces of your puzzle? What's YOUR vision? Write down the thoughts that come to mind.

_____

_____

_____

_____

_____

_____

_____

_____

_____

Ellegant Kickoff

To get you started, there are a few level-setting exercises I'd like you to work through.

Core Values Exercise

Before we get into Pillar 1 and look at your money values, I think it's important to visit (or revisit) your personal core values first. Vince Lombardi, at the beginning of every football training camp, held up a football and said, "Gentlemen, this is a football."[4] We too are going back to the basics first. (I promise this is the only sports analogy I'll use!)

If you are already crystal clear on your core values, you can skip to point number five below and go from there. If you haven't done this before or feel

---

[4] This Vince Lombardi quote used with permission of the Family of Vince Lombardi, c/o Luminary Group LLC, www.VinceLombardi.com. As head coach and general manager of the Green Bay Packers, Vince Lombardi led the team to three NFL championships and to victories in Super Bowls I and II (1967 and 1968). Because of his success, he became a national symbol of single-minded determination to win.

like going through the steps again, google "values exercise" and choose one of the exercises available. It should flow something like this:

1. There should be a long list of values for you to choose from.
2. Circle the twenty that really speak to you.
3. Sort them into four to six groups of values that have a similar meaning to you.
4. Within each grouping, select the one that stands out for you.
5. Those are your four to six core values.

Any surprises as you went through this? Did you select what you thought you *should* choose, or did you allow what really brings meaning to your life to rise to the top? Your definition of your core values could be different from someone else who decided on the same value.

Write down your core values and the meaning you attach to each one. For example, my top value is personal fulfillment, which to me means continual learning and following my true passion.

Core Value 1:

_____

Core Value 2:

_____

Core Value 3:

_____

Core Value 4:

_____

Core Value 5:

_____

Core Value 6:

_____

Financial Wellness Quiz

Go to https://www.ellegantwealth.com/EMPOWER and take the financial wellness quiz. Answer the twelve questions about your financial situation and get your score. Circle which personality represents you right now: blissfully unaware, definitely distressed, casually curious, or financially focused. Do this now and I'll have you take the quiz again at the end of the book. Hopefully, your fitness level will improve. 😊

The email you receive when you provide your name and email address will provide:

- A link to the quiz
- The 3 Step Guide to Shifting Your Money Mindset, which includes a list of additional resources
- The downloadable Net Worth Statement exercise you will complete in Pillar 3

Track Your Stock Exercise

The next exercise is to choose one stock (one company) you want to follow. There may be a sentimental reason for the stock choice. Maybe your grandfather worked at a company his entire career and you inherited some of that stock. Or, you have a favorite store you shop at on a regular basis. Whatever the reason, choose just one to follow as you read through the book.

Follow these steps (and don't worry, we will cover this terminology in more depth in Pillar 5 when we discuss investments—for now just follow the instructions):

1. Add the Stocks app, Yahoo Finance app, or something similar on your phone so you can easily monitor how your stock is doing.
2. You will need to find the ticker symbol for the company you've selected. Within the app, if you start typing in the name in the search bar, different ticker symbols will start to present themselves. You may have to do a little research to figure out the correct one. Some examples include MMM for 3M, AMZN for Amazon, AAPL for Apple.
3. Be sure it is a publicly traded company, meaning that it is a company that you can buy and sell on one of the stock exchanges. This is simply a place where stocks can be bought and sold. It cannot be

a privately held company whose stock is not traded in a way that you can easily follow the stock price.

4. Add this company to the list of stocks on your app so you can start to follow this company.

5. If you have an iPhone and are using the Stocks app, if you click on the ticker symbol for your stock, a chart will pop up so you can view how the stock price has been doing over different periods of time. Toward the bottom of that popup are recent headlines regarding that company.

6. Pay attention to what's happening with your company by monitoring the headline news.

It needs to be the right benchmark, not just any benchmark.

When you start keeping an eye on the moves in your company price, you will want to have a way to evaluate how well it is performing. One way to do that is to have a point of comparison or a benchmark.

What do I mean by a benchmark? Let me share a story to help you understand the concept.

I love going to the Minnesota State Fair every year at the end of August. I enjoy walking around and checking out the birthing barn, home project displays, boats, docks, and more. But, admittedly, my favorite part is the food. Like many people who go, I have my regulars—corn on the cob and deep-fried cheese curds always make the list. But the very last thing we do is stop at one of the Sweet Martha's booths to buy a bucket of chocolate chip cookies. It's overflowing with these warm, tasty little gems, and along with a glass of cold milk, we eat until we can get the cover on the bucket. Then we head to where the buses are all lined up and hop on ours to get back to our car and drive home. It's a fun excursion.

The rest of the year, anytime I have a chocolate chip cookie, I compare it to the Sweet Martha's cookies I get at the fair. That is my standard, my benchmark. Now, when I'm eating a blueberry muffin, I don't use Sweet Martha's cookies as the comparison. That wouldn't really make sense, would it? The benchmark you use to understand how your portfolio is performing is similar. It needs to be the right benchmark, not just any benchmark.

There are a multitude of investment benchmarks that are available. These are usually in the form of an index.

The Dow Jones Industrial Average (DJIA)[5], referred to as the Dow, is a common index made up of thirty blue-chip stocks, primarily large, healthy companies. It is often used as a gauge of the health of the market. When watching the news, you will hear reporters say, "The market was up twenty points today." They are typically referring to the Dow, even though it is only thirty companies.

The Standard & Poor's 500 Index (S&P 500), referred to as the S&P, is made up of five hundred large companies headquartered in the United States, comprising about 80% of the domestic equity market.

There are many more indexes, but these are two of the more common ones you will hear referred to in the news. They should already be listed in your Stocks app on your phone.

If you have a diversified portfolio of businesses that are primarily larger companies headquartered in the United States, the S&P 500 Index would be a good benchmark. The companies you own in that case would be comparable to the companies held in the index.

If you have a portfolio that consists primarily of companies that are headquartered in Europe, the S&P 500 Index would not be the appropriate benchmark because it is made up of U.S. (or domestic) companies. That would not be a good comparison to what you own.

As part of the exercise, I would also like to have you do the following tasks:

1. Write down the current value of the Dow and the S&P. For example, at the time I am writing this book, the Dow is valued at 28,195.42 and the S&P 500 at 3,426.92.
    - Today's Date _____
    - DJIA _____
    - S&P 500 _____

---

[5] Examples of companies in the DJIA are 3M, Apple, Coca-Cola, The Walt Disney Company, The Home Depot, McDonald's, Nike, Verizon, and Wal-Mart.

2. Write down the price of the one stock you have selected.
   - Your Stock _____
3. At the end of every pillar (chapter), I will ask you to write down the new values.
4. Similar to the items I asked you to pay attention to regarding the company you've chosen, do the same when it comes to what's happening in the economy and in the headline news. How do these events affect the Dow and the S&P 500? How do these events impact your stock?

It's not always intuitive. There are times it makes no sense whatsoever. You expect one reaction and something completely different happens. The market does not like uncertainty, so there may be an unexpected reaction if uncertainty presents itself. The market may also anticipate a certain outcome, so when it actually happens, the market doesn't react because it's already taken the event into consideration. Watch and see what you can learn about market behavior.

As soon as someone starts using terms we don't understand most of us shut down.

Every industry has its own language, but most of us don't need to understand it, so it doesn't really matter. There is a lot of jargon and lingo used in the investment world, and if we want to start to comprehend our financial situation, we need to figure out what this language means. As soon as someone starts using terms we don't understand, most of us shut down.

As you go through the book, if there is something you already know, that's great! Give yourself a pat on the back and move onto the next topic. Repetition is a great way to reinforce a concept. If you're not talking about this or using the terminology on a regular basis, it can be easy to forget the meaning. Allow yourself to review, refresh, and be delighted with any previous knowledge.

"Call it a clan, call it a network, call it a tribe, call it a family: Whatever you call it, whoever you are, you need one."
—Jane Howard, author

Ellegant Pillar 1: Explore Your Money Beliefs

Pillar 1 Key Concepts

1. Clarify what I value.
2. Increase my awareness around healthy money values.
3. Improve my ability to have open conversations around money.

"Marry a rich man." That's what my father told me over and over growing up. He would follow up with, "It's just as easy to fall in love with a rich man as it is a poor man." His second piece of wisdom was, "Go into sales. There's money to be had in sales." The message was clear—money was good; money would make my life better. Maybe you heard a similar message. Or, maybe you heard the complete opposite: money is bad; rich people are greedy or evil.

Take a moment to pause here and think about the money values and beliefs you grew up hearing.

Write your thoughts below:

_____

_____

_____

_____

_____

_____

_____

_____

_____

What you heard growing up is deeply embedded in your brain. As women, we're so busy taking care of everyone else, we rarely step back to give ourselves time and space to stop and think about the money values and beliefs we grew up hearing. Yet, we are often making decisions today based on those money messages we heard when we were young, and we don't even realize they are the basis for our decision.

Money intertwines with every aspect of our lives.

Money intertwines with every aspect of our lives. It impacts our relationships, careers, health and wellness, dreams, and communities.

Have you ever had a fight with a loved one over money? Yes, most of us have. It's very emotional. And yet, we often don't like to talk about it. Money is taboo. We'll talk about almost anything else with our friends, our family, our loved ones, but not money.

Money impacts our careers. If, like me, you grew up hearing money is good, you are probably driving for that next promotion and trying to make more money. If you heard money is bad, you might be sabotaging that promotion opportunity without even realizing why. But if you start making more money than anyone else in your family, you could be ostracized, like Uncle Bart, who was flashy and drove the fancy car.

Understanding why we approach money the way we do can improve how we communicate with other people in our lives and reduce the control money can have on us. I believe there is tremendous benefit in taking the time to understand the values we're carrying out in our lives.

It's about our legacy that we are going to leave behind. Do we genuinely want to pass on to our next generation the same money values and beliefs we grew up with? Or, is there something we want to change?

Ask a loved one what money values and beliefs they heard growing up. What stands out in their mind? You might be surprised by what you learn and the conversation it could spark. I've found that people love to share these memories given the opportunity. It's just so often we abide by the "money is taboo" barrier and never initiate the conversation. I dare you to give it a try!

MONEY
Values

Money Scripts | Money Beliefs | Money Blocks

- Derived from our earliest childhood.
- Deeply held.
- Unique to us.
- Play in the background.

Our money mindset can limit what's possible in our lives. We remember what we heard our parents talk about or fight about regarding money. There may have also been messages delivered by the refusal to talk about money.

Our money mindset can limit what's possible in our lives.

Everyone's beliefs are different—money is evil, money will give me meaning, there will never be enough money, money is unimportant, money is important. Draw your family tree with you at the center. Go up two generations, across to your partner and down as many generations you have. Think about the money values and beliefs that have been handed down to you. What are the memories, like my father telling me to marry a rich man, that come to mind? How are they contributing to how you feel about money and how you make decisions today? What are the money values and beliefs you're passing on to the next generations in your life? Are they the ones you want your family to attach to you? If not, what can you do to change that legacy? Start to connect the dots between what you heard and what you're doing.

Write your thoughts below:

_____

_____

_____

_____

_____

_____

_____

_____

_____

By tracking back two generations, you can really see how you got your values about money. It may be very scattered. It might feel like everyone was going in five different directions, and it was pure confusion. Or, there may have been very consistent messages and it's clear why you react to money the way you do. Are you the spender or the saver? Are you the one who gets into trouble or the one that bails everyone else out? We all have roles in our family dynamics.

Here are two examples of insights that women gained from going through this exercise.

Charlotte shared that she learned great things from her father about how to handle NOT having any money, which she appreciated. But it didn't help her figure out how to get money, how to make money, how to move up in the world. Her education lacked some vital components. But he didn't know how to teach her these things.

Another woman, Eve, had a mom who grew up very wealthy in a less-developed country, and when the existing government was overthrown, her family lost everything. As a result, her mom was obsessed with money and status and wanted to see their bank accounts grow. Her dad would pamper himself but hide it from her mom.

Her mother lived almost like she had lived in the Depression era, stocking up on necessities and balancing her checking account to the penny. As a result, Eve was a spender. She wanted to prove that she could be carefree about money. But when her mother passed away and she inherited the money her mother had painstakingly saved, she decided she wanted to be a good steward of this gift and, therefore, needed to learn more about managing finances.

Women like me, who had mothers who handled the finances, were more comfortable accepting that role. They didn't grow up seeing the man taking care of everything financial so didn't question their own capability. But that has certainly not been the norm for most women.

These roles can be deeply embedded.

These roles can be deeply embedded. What we observed growing up sticks with us. The question of who makes the financial decisions in the family can be difficult to change.

In the book *Storyselling for Financial Advisors: How Top Producers Sell*, Scott West and Mitch Anthony share the following:

"Individual values toward money and investing can vary greatly:

1. There are those who don't believe you can save enough, and there are those who believe you can't have enough to spend.
2. There are those who want to leave nothing to their heirs, and there are those who want to leave all they can to their heirs.

3. There are those who want to merely protect what they have, and there are those who want to 'roll the dice.'
4. There are those who want to retire as soon as possible, and there are those who plan on never retiring." [6]

What are your beliefs?
Write your thoughts below:

_____

_____

_____

_____

_____

_____

_____

_____

_____

---

[6] Scott West and Mitch Anthony, *Storyselling for Financial Advisors: How Top Producers Sell* (New York: Kaplan Publishing, 1999).

MONEY *Scripts*

- Money Avoidance
- Money Worship
- Money Status
- Money Vigilance
- From the Klontz Money Script Inventory (KMSI-R)
  https://www.moneyscripts.com

Go now and take the Klontz Money Script Inventory on https://www.moneyscripts.com or https://www.yourmental-wealthadvisors.com/our-process/your-money-script/.

Note: This link could change, so if you can't find it, google Klontz Money Script Inventory or moneyscripts. Also, some women have taken the inventory and then not received their results. If you don't receive your results within fifteen minutes, check your spam mailbox or go take it again.

Write your scores here:
Money Avoidance: _____
Money Worship: _____
Money Status: _____
Money Vigilance: _____,

Once you have your scores, read about the meaning behind each of the scripts.[7]

Money Avoidance: Money is bad, rich people are evil, I don't deserve money, sabotage opportunities to "move up," fear of being ostracized

Money Worship: Money will make me happier, money would solve all my problems, focus on things that will make more money not necessarily fulfillment or joy, workaholism

Money Status: Equate self-worth with net worth, as successful as amount of money made, focus on get-rich-quick schemes, gambling

Money Vigilance: Diligent, frugal, money should be saved not spent, won't spend money on training or education to do better or move up in career, incredibly focused on watching the balance in their accounts grow

My top scripts were money vigilance (something my husband finds hard to believe) and money worship. I've always lived within my means and saved for the future but also enjoyed making and spending money. This totally makes sense based on what I learned from each of my parents.

The diligence around money definitely came from my mom. She worked in the benefits and human resources department for a large company. When 401(k)s were first introduced, she immediately signed up. As she worked with the hourly laborers to enroll them in their benefits packages, she pushed each of them to do the same. I truly believe she changed the trajectory of many family's futures, although I'm sure most of them don't remember this quiet, small woman telling them what to do!

My dad was, as I've shared, telling me to marry a rich man and go into sales. He enjoyed spending money, even though we didn't have much. I remember when going to restaurants, we were all told to order whatever we wanted. We were never told to order the children's meal or get a hamburger instead of a steak. If we were going out, we were going all out and living large. My dad grew up in a family of twelve children and the money was limited. Saving for the future wasn't part of his plan. Money was meant to make life more enjoyable, and he was going to have fun with what he had at the moment.

---

[7] Brad Klontz and Rick Kahler 2016. *Facilitating Financial Health: Tools for Financial Planners, Coaches, and Therapists*, 2nd ed. (Cincinnati: National Underwriter Company, 2008): 80–81.

What were your scores and your top scripts? Do they make sense based on what you remember hearing growing up? Do you have family or friends who clearly identify with one of these scripts?

Write your thoughts below:

_____

_____

_____

_____

_____

_____

_____

_____

_____

Most of the women who have participated in my group coaching have found the results to be in line with what they expected. I did have one woman, however, who was completely baffled by the results. She said she was going to need to ponder this surprise for a bit.

In the article "The Stories We Tell About Money," Angie O'Leary shares, "Taking the time to identify your own money script can prove beneficial. Research suggests that understanding your money mindset and the circumstances that shaped your belief system helps facilitate financial health and leads to better outcomes."[8]

---

[8] Angie O'Leary. "The Stories We Tell About Money." LinkedIn, (2019), https://www.linkedin.com/pulse/stories-we-tell-money-angie-o-leary/.

I've also seen a lot of shame around money. It doesn't seem to matter if you have a lot of money or no money. I think some women who have money don't think they are deserving. They have difficulty admitting they have money. I remember a client I worked with, Val, who had a healthy estate but had a very real fear of becoming a bag lady. There was truly no reason for her to feel this way. There was no reason to believe the money they had amassed wouldn't last well beyond her and her husband's lifetime. Yet, in talking to her, it was obvious it was a concern she felt down to her bones. Nothing I said, none of the numbers I shared, made her feel better. She just couldn't seem to erase this childhood soundtrack from her memory. Something had happened to make her feel financially insecure, and no amount of money in her bank account could stop the movie from playing in her head.

Learning about money was a big step in moving forward.

If you have no money, there can be shame around that. Remember Charlotte? She worked incredibly hard but had so much stacked against her—family circumstances, coming from no means, the industry she was working in—it was going to be a battle to turn it around. But she was going to try. She was so beautiful and so proud. Learning about money was a big step in moving forward.

The Roles We Play

As women, we play a lot of roles. I don't think we always give ourselves credit for all the things we juggle. Write down some of the roles that represent who you are—wife, mother, daughter, sister, employee, business owner, volunteer, friend. There are also the multi-generational roles of taking care of parents, grandparents, children, and grandchildren. Seeing the list on paper is powerful. Thinking about the financial and emotional implications attached to each role can provide some "aha" moments.

As mothers, emotionally, there is tremendous joy and pride, along with exhaustion and fear. Financially, we may decide to take time out of, or scale back on, our careers. I'm not saying any particular decision is right or wrong, but there is a financial impact. It could mean different college choices for our children, pushing out our retirement, but it also means being more active in our children's lives.

As a wife, emotionally, there is love and companionship, along with re-sponsibilities and compromise. Financially, there may be a greater chance of building wealth, but there is also potentially greater financial stress. In partic-ular, if the two of you don't see eye to eye when it comes to spending and saving, there could be friction and arguments as a result.

I think each of these hats, each of these roles, comes with positive and negative considerations. It's about making choices—choices that are right for you, nobody else. Understanding the impact of those choices is what's valuable, laying out what happens if you make this choice versus that choice. But in the end, you do what works for you and your family.

It's about making choices—choices that are right for you, nobody else.

Role: _____ Emotional: _____ Financial: _____

Role: _____ Emotional: _____ Financial: _____

Role: _____ Emotional: _____ Financial: _____

Role: _____ Emotional: _____ Financial: _____

Role: _____ Emotional: _____ Financial: _____

Role: _____ Emotional: _____ Financial: _____

Ellegant
PILLAR
WRAP UP

Wrap Up Exercise: Pillar 1, Explore Your Money Beliefs

Take a moment and think about what surprises or "aha" moments you've experienced as a result of reading Pillar 1 and doing the exercises.

Write your thoughts below:

_____

_____

_____

_____

_____

_____

_____

_____

What would be one or two small steps you could take to move forward on your journey?

Write your thoughts below:

_____

_____

_____

_____

_____

_____

_____

_____

Track Your Stock

Write down the price of the stock and the value of the DJIA and S&P 500:

Today's Date _____

        DJIA _____

        S&P 500 _____

        Your Stock _____

How is your stock doing? Is it up or down from when you first wrote down the stock price?

Write your thoughts below:

_____

_____

_____

_____

_____

_____

_____

_____

_____

Consider these questions:

1. What news has been in the headlines recently?
   a. Political issues? Global issues? Environmental issues? Has the Federal Reserve been making any changes?
2. What has been happening with the overall market?
   a. Have the S&P 500 and DJIA been up or down?
   b. Has there been a lot of volatility or has it been relatively steady?
3. How has this been impacting your stock?
   a. Has it been up or down?
   b. Has it been tracking with the market or moving differently?
4. How do you feel about this?
   a. Comfortable, anxious, happy, sad?
   b. Has this provided any insights into your risk tolerance?

Write your thoughts below:

_____

_____

_____

_____

_____

_____

_____

_____

_____

You will be prompted to do this same exercise at the end of each pillar.

Ellegant
PILLAR 2
Establish Your Financial Goals

"The future belongs to those who believe in the beauty of their dreams."
—Eleanor Roosevelt, former first lady

Ellegant Pillar 2: Establish Your Financial Goals

Pillar 2 Key Concepts

1. Define what I want to achieve with my money.
2. Embrace my goals with enthusiasm and intention.
3. Create a plan for my future.

We forget to focus on ourselves.

What's your destination? What is it you want to achieve? Have you ever really stopped to think about what's important to you? As women, we're often so busy taking care of everyone else and making sure everyone else is happy, we forget to focus on ourselves. This is your chance to first dream and then set the goals and steps so you can move forward on your journey.

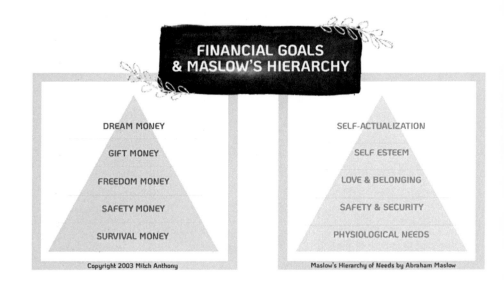

FINANCIAL GOALS & MASLOW'S HIERARCHY

DREAM MONEY	SELF-ACTUALIZATION
GIFT MONEY	SELF ESTEEM
FREEDOM MONEY	LOVE & BELONGING
SAFETY MONEY	SAFETY & SECURITY
SURVIVAL MONEY	PHYSIOLOGICAL NEEDS

Copyright 2003 Mitch Anthony   Maslow's Hierarchy of Needs by Abraham Maslow

"The greater danger for most of us isn't that our aim is too high and we miss it, but that it is too low and we reach it."
—Michelangelo, Italian sculptor

You might be familiar with Maslow's hierarchy of needs.[9] Mitch Anthony writes in his book, *The New Rementality,* about our hierarchy of financial needs, calling it "Maslow Meets Retirement."[10] I thought this was a wonderful comparison (see image above).

1. Survival money consists of needs such as groceries and mortgage or rent, which is equivalent to physiological needs on Maslow's scale.
2. Safety money includes health and life insurance, akin to safety and security on Maslow's hierarchy.
3. Freedom money consists of activities or items that bring joy, such as travel and fine wine. This equates to love and belonging on Maslow's scale.

---

[9] Abraham Maslow. "A Theory of Human Motivation." *Psychological Review,* vol. 50, issue 4 (1943): 370–396, https://doi.org/10.1037/h0054346.
[10] Mitch Anthony. *The New Rementality: Planning Your Life and Living Your Dreams...At Any Age You Want*, 4th ed. (Nashville, TN: John Wiley & Sons, 2014).

4. Gift money is what you can give to the people and causes close to your heart. Compare this to self-esteem on the hierarchy of needs.
5. Dream money allows us to do what we want to do—what brings you true happiness and meaning, and compares to self-actualization.

Survival Money

When I first started working, I was making $13,000 a year, and I had $12,000 of student debt, so I was happy to have survival money. Fortunately, I worked for a good company and had insurance, so that provided the safety aspect as well. Even though I could barely make ends meet, I was contributing to the company 401(k) plan. My mother had drilled into me the importance of saving for the future. I started with whatever percentage the company was matching, and each year, when I received a raise, I increased the percentage. I did this until I reached the maximum and never stopped contributing the maximum after that.

Encourage the young people in your life to start investing in their future as early as possible.

Freedom Money

As my husband and I continued to move up in our careers, we were able to travel more and buy our cabin.

Gift Money

We were able to help our son with college and a home purchase. We have also been blessed to be able to give to charities we care about.

Dream Money

Following my passion to start my company and helping women in a meaningful way is absolutely my dream. Because both my husband and I started saving early by contributing to our 401(k) plans, I felt I we had the foundation that allowed me to do this. I know I am incredibly blessed to have this opportunity, and I'm grateful every day that this is what I get to do!

Some women shared they felt the order was different for them—it wasn't experienced in a linear fashion. This tended to be the more creative, right-brained women. My analytical, left-brain thinking has often led me to be very linear in my approach, but we are always moving up, down, and around. Experiencing a loss of a loved one or having a financial windfall could move you to a different point on the pyramid. Feel free to view the pyramid in a more fluid fashion that works for you.

Take a moment to dream.

Where do you fall on the pyramid? Where are you in this journey? If you were to reach the pinnacle, what does that look like to you? Take a moment to dream. Allow yourself the pleasure.

Write your thoughts below:

_____

_____

_____

_____

_____

_____

_____

_____

_____

I worked with a life coach who shared a wonderful analogy with me. If you think about your future as a garden, what seeds do you want to nurture and what weeds do you want to pull? Start to envision the beautiful garden you'll have if you pay more attention to what you truly want. What's in your garden?

Write your thoughts below:

_____

_____

_____

_____

_____

_____

_____

_____

_____

_____

Set SMARTER goals AND write them down!

Specific
Measurable
Action-Oriented
Risky
Time-Stamped
Exciting
Relevant

Source: Michael Hyatt

"Outside of your comfort zone is where the magic happens."
—Unknown

I'm a huge fan of Michael Hyatt! He's a productivity guru. I use his full focus planner and have read his book *Your Best Year Ever*.[11] I like his methodology of SMARTER goals (see image above). In the business world, SMART goals are common (specific, measurable, action-oriented, relevant, time-stamped). I love the addition of risky and exciting.

Goals that make you light up when you talk about them.

Often in the corporate world, you have goals that are given to you. You don't necessarily choose them. The goals we're talking about here are the

---

[11] Michael Hyatt. *Your Best Year Ever: A 5-Step Plan for Achieving Your Most Important Goals*. (Ada, OK: Baker Books, 2018).

goals you want to achieve. Goals that make you light up when you talk about them. They are exciting goals you will work hard to achieve.

What are those goals for you? And why do want to achieve them?
Write your thoughts below:

_____

_____

_____

_____

_____

_____

_____

_____

_____

You need to truly understand the "why" behind your goals. Be sure you have clearly articulated the "why." When you hit the messy middle and the going gets tough (and it will), you will need to come back to the "why" to help you push through to the end. Simon Sinek has a fantastic TEDTalk called "How Great Leaders Inspire Action." In it, he explains the meaning behind the "why."[12] Worth a look.

---

[12] Simon Sinek. "How Great Leaders Inspire Action." TEDTalks, (2009), https://www.ted.com/talks/simon_sinek_how_great_leaders_inspire_action. This book is not being officially endorsed by Simon Sinek or Simon Sinek Inc. You may find additional resources at www.simonsinek.com.

I have always been a goal setter and a planner. My senior year in college, I set two goals. I wanted to work for an airline, and I wanted to start my master's in business administration (MBA) within two years of completing college. The first goal was because my mom took me on a trip to Portugal my senior year in high school and I got the travel bug. The

WRITE IT DOWN!

second goal was partly because my brother had accomplished that (and if he could, I could too) and partly because I saw it as a path to more money.

When I graduated from college, I had two job offers—the first as a reservations agent at Northwest Airlines and the second as a corporate treasury analyst at Republic Airlines (Republic). I had interviewed for many other positions, but these were the only two offers I received. Was it because of the goal I set and put out into the world? Not sure, but I happily accepted the job with Republic. The benefits were amazing. I could hop on any of their flights for $5 one way in coach or $15 one way in first class, if there was a seat available on stand-by. My parents, spouse, and children received the same benefits. Now the drawback was I didn't have any vacation or any money. But my mom loved to travel, so we made numerous weekend trips around the United States. We went to Atlanta, Boston, New York, and more.

Eighteen months into my stint in my industry of choice, Republic was purchased by Northwest Airlines. My boss jumped ship, and I was offered the equivalent of his job at Northwest. I had been interviewing with Cargill, Inc. and was offered a position in their corporate treasury group that was basically a lateral move. I took the job with Cargill. Go back to the two goals I set in college. Northwest had no tuition reimbursement program, and Cargill offered full tuition reimbursement. As much as I had enjoyed getting to work in the airline industry, the part of me that wanted to make more money was stronger, and I felt I had to get the advanced degree to continue to move up the corporate ladder.

WRITE IT DOWN! The article "One of the Best Steps You Can Take to Retire Wealthy Can Be Done Today," cites a study by Schwab that states that we are 60% more likely to increase our savings and twice as likely to stick with a savings plan if we write it down.[13] Only 24% of the people surveyed said they had a written plan. Neuroscience also suggests that if we write down our goals, we are more likely to follow through. A different part of the brain lights up when you write goals down, causing those goals to be more memorable. Putting pen to paper is important.

But don't go overboard. Dreaming of writing a best-selling novel is wonderful, but setting a goal to spend fifteen minutes a day writing is a great starting point. Look at making bite-sized changes; don't try to eat the elephant all at one time.

What are some of the goals you'd like to achieve? Have you written down goals in the past? If setting goals is new, what surprises or roadblocks did you run into as you worked through the process? What can you do to overcome any issues? What are different approaches you could take?

Spend some time brainstorming and talking to friends and family members about what you want to achieve. You might be surprised at the ideas and support you receive.

---

[13] Walter Upgrave. "One of the Best Steps You Can Take to Retire Wealthy Can Be Done Today," realdealretirement.com, (2017), https://realdealretirement.com/this-simple-exercise-can-dramatically-improve-your-retirement-prospects/.

Write your thoughts below:

_____

_____

_____

_____

_____

_____

_____

_____

Wrap Up Exercise: Pillar 2, Establish Your Financial Goals

Take a moment and think about what surprises or "aha" moments you've experienced as a result of reading Pillar 2 and doing the exercises.

Write your thoughts below:

_____

_____

_____

_____

_____

_____

_____

_____

What would be one or two small steps you could take to move forward on your journey?

Write your thoughts below:

_____

_____

_____

_____

_____

_____

_____

_____

_____

Track Your Stock

Write down the price of the stock and the value of the DJIA and S&P 500:

Today's Date _____

DJIA _____

S&P 500 _____

Your Stock _____

How is your stock doing? Is it up or down from when you first wrote down the stock price?

Write your thoughts below:

_____

_____

_____

_____

_____

_____

_____

_____

_____

Consider these questions:

1. What news has been in the headlines recently?
    a. Political issues? Global issues? Environmental issues? Has the Federal Reserve been making any changes?
2. What has been happening with the overall market?
    a. Have the S&P 500 and DJIA been up or down?
    b. Has there been a lot of volatility or has it been relatively steady?
3. How has this been impacting your stock?
    a. Has it been up or down?
    b. Has it been tracking with the market or moving differently?
4. How do you feel about this?
    a. Comfortable, anxious, happy, sad?
    b. Has this provided any insights into your risk tolerance?

Write your thoughts below:

_____

_____

_____

_____

_____

_____

_____

_____

_____

Know Your Net Worth

*"Find something you're passionate about and keep
tremendously interested in it."*
—Julia Child, chef

Ellegant Pillar 3: Know Your Net Worth

Pillar 3 Key Concepts

1. Gain visibility into my resources, allowing me to plan what I can achieve (or accomplish).
2. Provide a measurement that will help me gauge my financial progress.
3. Believe that my net worth does not define my self-worth.

To arrive at your destination (the goals we talked about in Pillar 2), you need to know your starting point. There will be a variety of ways you could get there—planes, trains, and automobiles—maybe you'll take all three and maybe you'll need more—bicycles and kayaks. The map to get there will likely change along the way.

I remember when my husband and I decided to go to Cozumel, Mexico, on vacation. I booked our flights from Minneapolis to Cancun. From Cancun, we took a bus to Playa del Carmen. We then dragged our luggage a few blocks through town to get to the ferry. Of course, we had just missed it, so we had a drink while we waited. We took the ferry to Cozumel and grabbed a taxi to the resort. It took us all day to make this trek (and we were both a *little* crabby along the way).

Keep in mind, the path is not always direct.

At some point during our stay, we discovered we could have flown directly into Cozumel from Minneapolis (I'm sure for a little more money). We ended up taking a flight from Cozumel to Cancun on the way back, which was worth every penny!

Keep in mind, the path is not always direct.

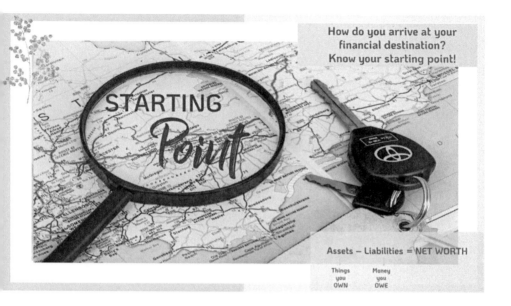

Assets – Liabilities = NET WORTH

| Things you OWN | Money you OWE |

Do you know how much your home is worth? How much debt you have? How much money is in your investment accounts? How much you need to retire?

It's difficult to arrive at your destination if you don't know your starting point.

It's difficult to arrive at your destination if you don't know your starting point. When you're booking a flight to your favorite vacation spot, you need to know both your destination and your starting point.

It's like the sign at the shopping mall that reads, "You are Here!" Knowing your net worth, what tax bracket you're in, the approximate amount of insurance coverage you have, and having a will and estate plan in place are all valuable pieces of information, all necessary pieces of the puzzle you are putting together.

Your assets are things you own. They can be your home, investments, retirement accounts, or savings. What is the value of each of those assets at this point in time? List all of those things on a piece of paper or in a spreadsheet with the value next to it. Add up the total value of those assets.

Your liabilities are things such as the balances you owe on your mortgage, vehicles, and credit cards. List all of those items along with the amount owed at this point in time and add them up.

Now, take your assets minus your liabilities and that equals your net worth. This is the indicator of how wealthy you are financially.

The next two pages provide additional thoughts (but by no means is all-inclusive) of assets and liabilities to be considered (Step 1) as well as an example of how you would put together your net worth statement (Step 2). If you took the quiz in the kickoff section, you have already received the email with both of these pages in a printable format. If you didn't, go to https://www.elle-gantwealth.com/EMPOWER and get your goodies!

GATHER YOUR "STUFF"

ASSETS

Bank account statements
- *Checking*
- *Savings*
- *Money market*

Investment account statements
- *All personal investment accounts*

Retirement account statements
- *Roth IRA accounts*
- *401(k) accounts*
- *Rollover IRA accounts*

Life insurance cash value
- *Term policies*
- *Whole life policies*

Personal property values (current)
- *Cars*
- *Jewelry*
- *Art*

Residential real estate values
- *Primary home*
- *Vacation homes*
- *Other*

Loans you have made to others
- *Miscellaneous/Other assets*

LIABILITIES

Credit card balances

Loan balances
- *Home mortgage*
- *Other mortgages*
- *Home equity line of credit (HELOC)*
- *Car loans*
- *Student loans*
- *Loans against life insurance or 401(k)*
- *Other debt*

CREATE YOUR NET WORTH STATEMENT

ASSETS	VALUE ($)
• Bank Accounts	
• Investment Accounts	
• Retirement Accounts	
• Real Estate/Property	
• Life Insurance Cash Values	
• Personal Assets	
• Miscellaneous/Other	
TOTAL ASSETS	

LIABILITIES	VALUE ($)
• Credit Card Balances	
• Home Mortgages	
• Other Mortgages	
• Consumer Loans	
• Home Equity Line of Credit (HELOC)	
• Student Loans	
• Car Loans	
• Loans Against Life Insurance/401(k)	
• Other Debt	

TOTAL ASSETS - TOTAL LIABILITIES = NET WORTH

Our net worth does not define us.

This is where you begin, your starting point. Understanding your net worth allows you to move toward accomplishing your money goals.

You may have a net-worth statement that your financial advisor provided for you. Feel free to use that for this exercise if you'd like, but take the time to truly look at it and think about everything that's listed. Having an awareness and understanding of your net worth is what we're really trying to get at here. Don't just skip past this step because you have the answer in hand.

What I've found, working with clients, is unless you actually take the time to dig into this, you forget things. When someone else puts it together, you don't give it the same attention. So spend some time on this. I've found when you really pay attention to it, you want to see every asset listed. Suddenly, you remember things that didn't come to mind when someone else did the work for you.

How do you think your net worth impacts your ability to achieve your goals? Have your money values and beliefs influenced the size of your net worth? Look back at Pillars 1 and 2. View your net-worth statement through the lens of your values and your goals. Are there changes you could make to get all of these in better alignment? Or, does everything match up beautifully?

Write your thoughts below:

_____

_____

_____

_____

_____

_____

_____

_____

My grandmother, who had twelve children, fifty grandchildren, hundreds of great and great-great grandchildren always said she was rich in love, and she truly was. Always remember your net worth does not equate to your self-worth. Our net worth does not define us—it's just a tool to help us achieve our goals.

What are your priceless assets? The gifts that make you special and unique? It's really powerful to take the time to honor yourself. We do it far too little.

I believe some of my gifts include my ability to connect with people, to relate to their situation, to see what makes them unique, and to make them feel special.

This was hard for me to write, as it may be for many of you. I can think of situations in which I have not done any of these things well. And of course, it's always easier to dwell on the times we fell short. But most of the time, I know these are my strengths, and like all of us, I need to embrace them and forgive myself when I don't live up to my own expectations.

Write down your priceless assets and share them with someone else.

Write your thoughts below:

_____

_____

_____

_____

_____

_____

_____

_____

_____

_____

THE *Future*

1 **Pay yourself first.**
   Automate as much as you can (i.e. Traditional 401k)

2 **Create an emergency "curve ball" fund so you are prepared for the unexpected.**

Money Saving & Finance Apps

acorns

CAPITAL

digit

PERSONAL CAPITAL

"Don't save what is left after spending but spend what is left after saving." — Warren Buffett

"Don't save what is left after spending but spend what is left after saving."
—Warren Buffett, chairman and CEO of Berkshire Hathaway

Be *proactive* with your money, not reactive.

You need to plan TODAY for the future! Be *proactive* with your money, not reactive.

This particular information may not apply specifically to you or your situation, depending on where you're at financially. But I think it's important to know this anyway so you can have conversations with your children, grandchildren, nieces, and nephews and help them understand these concepts.

It used to be people retired at sixty-five after forty years with the same company. They figured they'd live another ten years and were relying on a combination of a pension, social security, and modest savings to get them through their lifetime. You may not have seen your parents saving money for retirement because they didn't think it was necessary. It also means they didn't teach you how to save or talk about why it was important to save.

Now it seems the expectation for young people is they only want to work thirty to thirty-five years. They could then be retired for that same amount of time. Pensions have become pretty much nonexistent. The thought around social security is that it will likely be gone by the time they retire, or at least I certainly wouldn't depend on that as a significant part of the plan. They will need to save in a much bigger way than the generations before them.

Think about it this way: for each year they work, they are paying for one year of today's lifestyle AND one year of retirement.

We need to educate them and help them prepare for their future! For example, make sure they are contributing to a 401(k) plan if they work for a public or private company, 403(b) if they work for a public school, or 457(b) if they work for a state or local government.

At the very least, encourage them to take advantage of the company match, if offered. The company match is when the organization offers to match your withholding. The percentage match will differ, but if it's 4%, you are in essence receiving a 4% bonus, just by smartly pushing 4% of your salary into the retirement plan they offer. Please don't pass this up or let anyone you care about pass this up!

If there isn't access to a 401(k), contributing to an individual retirement account (IRA) is the next best option. There are restrictions around contributions amounts for both of these options.

Depending on income level, it could make more sense to be utilizing the benefit of a Roth 401(k) or Roth IRA, rather than going the traditional route. This is a more in-depth conversation than we are going to get into here, but worth researching or talking about with an advisor.

When investing in a traditional 401(k) or IRA, the contribution takes place before paying taxes on the money. If you are in a high tax bracket, this is a way to reduce the taxes you pay and tuck money away pre-tax. When investing in a Roth 401(k) or IRA, you pay the taxes and then make the contribution. If you are in a lower tax bracket, this may be the route to take.

In both situations, the money grows tax free. However, when you decide to make a distribution to yourself from the traditional 401(k) or IRA, you will now pay taxes on both the original pre-tax contribution as well as the growth that has taken place. The idea is that you will be in a lower tax bracket when you are retired than you were when you were working, reducing the amount of taxes paid.

In the Roth 401(k) or IRA, you have already paid the taxes on the original contribution and all withdrawals 'are tax free. This is a great option for individuals in a lower tax bracket. Even if you are in a higher tax bracket, you may want to consider splitting your contribution between the traditional and the Roth.

What can happen if you only contribute to the traditional option is the taxes can be a concern if this is a significant portion of your retirement assets. Unfortunately, for many of us in or nearing retirement, the traditional was the only option available to us during most of our careers. The Roth 401(k) didn't come on the scene until 2006, and many companies didn't offer this option until much later.

One thing to consider after you retire, or at any time you move into a lower tax bracket, is what's called a Roth conversion. This is a situation where you transition your traditional assets into a Roth. There is a lot to consider in that type of scenario, so this is a great conversation for you to have with your advisor or tax accountant.

There are also tax consequences and penalties to be aware of with regards to 401(k)s and IRAs.

Another topic for younger adults, starting a family or with young children, is a 529 plan (or education savings plan). This is also something for grandparents to consider starting for their grandchildren.

We had a close family member have a baby. I wrote out a check and put it in the card with a note that I wanted the gift to go into a 529 plan for the baby. The young couple had no idea what I was talking about. I took the opportunity to teach them about the value of starting to save for college early.

If possible, having money automatically contributed to a 529 plan each month is ideal. Consider starting with $25 a month and each year doubling or increasing the amount. It could mean putting any monetary gifts received from family members or friends for the child into the account. The 529 plan allows money you have already paid taxes on to grow tax free. If used for educational tuition (that follow certain rules), there are no federal tax implications (state rules vary, so please check into your specific state). There are additional rules and things to understand here, but again, I'm going to let you do some research or ask your financial advisor or planner about this as well.

Everyone should be paying themselves first.

Another thing to consider is if you save $50 a day for twenty years and get an average 10% return (which is a pretty aggressive goal), you will have $1 million at the end of the twenty years! In a workshop I held, some of the women said there was no way they could save $50 a day, but they were going to start with $10 a day or $25 a day. Whatever works for you, start somewhere.

Everyone should be paying themselves first. I have to admit, for a long time, I didn't understand what that meant. The best way to accomplish this is to automate your savings. If you never see it, you're far less likely to spend it. It's contributing to a retirement plan at work or an IRA like we've just covered. Direct a portion of your check to an investment account or education savings plan. Do whatever it takes to move 20% of your income or as much as you can into accounts that you don't look at regularly. Keep this money out of your checking and savings accounts.

It is also a good idea to have an emergency fund (or curveball account) tucked away, out of sight if possible. We all have emergencies happen—the furnace goes out on the coldest night of the year, your house is hit by lightning and you have to front the replacement of the appliances before receiving the insurance proceeds—things that happened to my family. So be prepared for the unexpected and give yourself a cushion. This is typically three to six months of income or whatever amount will make you feel comfortable. Start small. You won't arrive immediately, but plan and you will get there.

Wrap Up Exercise: Pillar 3, Know Your Net Worth

Take a moment and think about what surprises or "aha" moments you've experienced as a result of reading Pillar 3 and doing the exercises.

Write your thoughts below:

_____

_____

_____

_____

_____

_____

_____

Track Your Stock

Write down the price of the stock and the value of the DJIA and S&P 500:

Today's Date _____

      DJIA _____

      S&P 500 _____

      Your Stock _____

How is your stock doing? Is it up or down from when you first wrote down the stock price?

Write your thoughts below:

_____

_____

_____

_____

_____

_____

_____

Consider these questions:

1. What news has been in the headlines recently?
   a. Political issues? Global issues? Environmental issues? Has the Federal Reserve been making any changes?
2. What has been happening with the overall market?
   a. Have the S&P 500 and DJIA been up or down?
   b. Has there been a lot of volatility or has it been relatively steady?
3. How has this been impacting your stock?
   a. Has it been up or down?
   b. Has it been tracking with the market or moving differently?
4. How do you feel about this?
   a. Comfortable, anxious, happy, sad?
   b. Has this provided any insights into your risk tolerance?

Write your thoughts below:

Ellegant
PILLAR
4

Spend With Purpose

"When you invest, you are buying a day that you don't have to work."
—Aya Laraya, speaker and investment advocate

Ellegant Pillar 4: Spend with Purpose

Pillar 4 Key Concepts

1. Improve skills to make informed financial decisions.
2. Ability to take control of my finances and live the life I desire.
3. Make choices that are deliberate and purposeful when it comes to spending money.

Tomorrow's Treasures, Past Promises, and Today's Joy

I'm not a fan of the "b" word—budget. What word did you think I was going to say? It's a word that reminds me of diet. It feels like a punishment. I don't really want to go on a diet or a budget, and I'm going to do it for as short a time as possible.

If you can create a budget and stick with it, that's wonderful! I've found most people have a hard time following or maintaining a budget. Then they feel like they've failed.

Systematic, automatic, continual savings will get you to your financial goals in the most pain-free process possible. Getting money tucked away in a retirement account, like a 401(k) or IRA, or 529 education savings plan so you don't even have access to the money is the ideal method. Having the money swept right into the investment vehicle will provide the best opportunity for success.

I do think it's helpful to take a broad brush to your current spending. The approach I encourage using breaks your expenses into three categories:

- Tomorrow's Treasures: What are you saving for the future (retirement, family adventure, college tuition)?
- Past Promises: What commitments have you already made (mortgage or rent, utilities, car payment)?
- Today's Joy: What is left over after tomorrow's treasures and past promises (dining out, designer clothes, theater tickets)?

Systematic, automatic continual savings will get you to your financial goals in the most pain-free process possible.

Many women spend a lot of time thinking about and working on their health and wellness. To achieve and maintain a healthy lifestyle, you need to pay attention to your decisions every day. You want to get daily movement, eat healthy meals, get enough sleep, practice gratitude and mindfulness, and so on. That is what it takes to perform self-care from a holistic perspective.

What's often neglected or overlooked is financial wellness. It requires a similar focus. You can't look at your spending once a year and expect to be on track with your plan. Your money needs to be a consistent aspect of your life: paying attention to what you're spending and how it makes you feel. Ask yourself if it's in alignment with your values. You need to develop a healthy relationship with money because we have almost daily interactions with money, whether buying groceries, buying a house, or paying the bills.

> What's often neglected or overlooked is financial wellness.

I would encourage you to view financial wellness as part of your overall personal wellness plan.

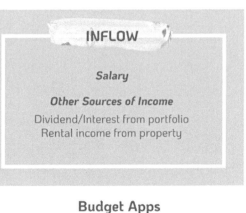

INFLOW

Salary

Other Sources of Income
Dividend/Interest from portfolio
Rental income from property

Budget Apps

mint everydollar **YNAB.** claritymoney

You can decide to be successful with money—the key word here is DECIDE. Going back to the diet analogy, we all know what we need to do to be successful when it comes to physical wellness: eat less and exercise more. When it comes to fiscal fitness, we all know what it takes to make it work: spend less and save more.

This is HARD! Nobody is saying this is fun or easy. It doesn't matter if you're making $1 million a year or $50,000 a year. This applies to everyone. If you're spending more than you make, it doesn't work. You do the math.

It's all about choices.

Understanding your cash flow is key here. To calculate your cash flow, you take the cash inflows minus the cash outflows. The goal is to arrive at a positive number!

Your cash inflows are any sources of income you are receiving: your salary from a job or your business, dividend and interest income from investment accounts, or rental income from any properties you own. There are a variety of ways to bring in money. Often, it requires hard work. It might be multiple jobs. But increasing the cash inflow is one of the easiest ways to increase the bottom line.

Spending *Thoughtfully*

How much is coming in and how much is going out?

OUTFLOW

Tomorrow's Treasures
Family Adventures, Retirement, New Business, Charity, Legacy

Past Promises
Mortgage, Car payment, Insurance

Today's Joy
Eating out, Facials, Theatre, Hobbies

Good Old Taxes

Your cash outflows equal your spending. This is a big, long list. It includes everything and anything that takes your money.

- Tomorrow's Treasures
  - This is any money you're tucking away for the future.
    - Retirement accounts, educations savings account, investment accounts
    - Money set aside for big family adventures, a new business, charity, etc.
  - Ideally, this is about 20% of your cash inflow.
- Past Promises
  - These are monetary commitments you've already made.
    - Mortgage or rent payment, car payment, insurance, utilities, etc.
  - Ideally, this is about 50% of your cash inflow, but depending on where you live and your lifestyle, it could be higher or lower.
- Today's Joy
  - This is just like it sounds, the stuff that brings immediate joy!
    - Dining out, travel, theater, hobbies, etc.
  - This amount should be about 30% of your cash inflow but depends heavily on tomorrow's treasures and past promises.

The key here is FIRST getting money into tomorrow's treasures. Second, planning thoughtfully with regards to past promises. Third, having money left to enjoy now!

This goes back to the Warren Buffet quote. Don't spend first and save later. It rarely works.

Think about some of the areas where you tend to spend large amounts during the year, like dining out or travel, and consider prioritizing what's truly important to you. Are there changes you could make that would have a significant impact? If you really love to travel, maybe you eliminate or reduce how often you go out for dinner. Or, maybe you start packing a lunch. Choose the tradeoffs that work for you. But spend the time thinking and planning what these shifts look like for you.

Write your thoughts below:

_____

_____

_____

_____

_____

_____

_____

_____

_____

The article "Buying Time Promotes Happiness," shares that "individuals who spend money on time-saving services report greater life satisfaction."[14]

I love getting my house cleaned—and based on what women have shared with me, that seems to be the number one answer. Other examples are getting the lawn mowed or having your meals prepared. Is there something you would like to get off your plate? Maybe that's a goal for your future.

Write your thoughts below:

_____

_____

_____

_____

_____

_____

_____

_____

_____

---

[14] Ashley Whillans, Elizabeth Dunn, Paul Smeets, Rene Bekkers, and Michael Norton. "Buying Time Promotes Happiness." *Proceedings of the National Academy of Sciences of the United States of America* vol. 114 issue 32 (2017): 8523–27, https://www.pnas.org/content/early/2017/07/18/1706541114.

Spend time understanding your cashflow. Make a list of your inflows. Track your outflows. Use whatever format, spreadsheets, or apps that work for you. Go high level or go deep. Do whatever you think will help you get your arms around how you spend.

What discoveries did you make? Were you surprised by anything? Does your spending fit with your money values? What changes are you going to make to help you achieve your goals?

Write your thoughts below:

_____

_____

_____

_____

_____

_____

_____

_____

_____

I know this can be really hard. Of course you don't want to give up anything you enjoy. But being more conscious around your spending and doing less of the "feel good," "gives me a quick hit," "retail therapy" spending will have longer-term rewards. Increased awareness provides amazing clarity and will allow you to make better choices.

Of course you don't want to give up
anything you enjoy.

Wrap Up Exercise: Pillar 4, Spend with Purpose

Take a moment and think about what surprises or "aha" moments you've experienced as a result of reading Pillar 4 and doing the exercises.

Write your thoughts below:

_____

_____

_____

_____

_____

_____

_____

What would be one or two small steps you could take to move forward on your journey?

Write your thoughts below:

_____

_____

_____

_____

_____

_____

_____

_____

_____

Track Your Stock

Write down the price of the stock and the value of the DJIA and S&P 500:

Today's Date _____
DJIA _____
S&P 500 _____
Your Stock _____

How is your stock doing? Is it up or down from when you first wrote down the stock price?

Write your thoughts below:

_____
_____
_____
_____
_____
_____
_____
_____
_____

Consider these questions:

1. What news has been in the headlines recently?
   a. Political issues? Global issues? Environmental issues? Has the Federal Reserve been making any changes?
2. What has been happening with the overall market?
   a. Have the S&P 500 and DJIA been up or down?
   b. Has there been a lot of volatility or has it been relatively steady?
3. How has this been impacting your stock?
   c. Has it been up or down?
   d. Has it been tracking with the market or moving differently?
4. How do you feel about this?
   c. Comfortable, anxious, happy, sad?
   d. Has this provided any insights into your risk tolerance?

Write your thoughts below:

_____

_____

_____

_____

_____

_____

_____

_____

_____

Learn To Speak "Investments"

"I'm nicer when I like my outfit."
—Unknown

Ellegant Pillar 5: Learn to Speak "Investments"

Pillar 5 Key Concepts

1. Discover I am capable of comprehending financial concepts and jargon.
2. Recognize that managing my finances is like managing my health—I have to be involved.
3. Understand the risks and rewards of investing so I can make informed decisions for my financial future.

We've reached my favorite pillar! I love investments, and I want you to love investments too (well, okay, at least have an interest). I hear people say investments are frustrating, intimidating, and boring. I don't think they are any of those things, and I don't want you to feel that way either. This is the chance to shift that thinking.

I want you to be actively participating in the discussion about your financial future and it's hard to accomplish that if you don't understand investments.

Girls and boys have historically been raised differently when it comes to money. Boys are often taught about investing and girls about saving and giving. While I think saving and giving are wonderful and should absolutely be applauded, women also need to know how to invest. Now, I'm not suggesting you fire your advisor and take over the reins. I want you to be actively participating in the discussion about your financial future and it's hard to accomplish that if you don't understand investments.

My friend Jasmine asked me one day, "Why do you love investments so much?" There are so many reasons, but first on the list would have to be the power of investing. If you look back at the stock market's history, it has steadily gone up over time. Yes, there have been significant drops at different times, but it has always come back and then exceeded previous highs.

As an investment professional, one of the things that was always drilled into me is, "Past performance is not an indicator of future performance." But if I saved my money and put it under my mattress or deposited it in a savings account, I wouldn't have even kept up with inflation. My money would have eroded in value if I did in essence nothing but save. Investing in a thoughtful fashion, over time, has allowed my money to grow in value.

I also think investing is intellectually challenging. You can't predict what's going to happen in the various markets. You can make forecasts based on logical reasoning and thorough analysis, but nobody has the perfect crystal ball. Things happen to throw it off course, like political events—in the United States and globally—that can't be anticipated. I've often wondered if it's this lack of knowing you are making the "right" choice that is preventing people from making any choice.

Investing also provides me with a sense of security about my current and future financial situation. You may be thinking to yourself, *What? That is completely counterintuitive to how I feel.* Investments are a tool that can make my hard-earned money grow, which can, in turn, provide financial independence and the ability to achieve financial goals.

You also get to own part of a company through investing. Many people will never decide to start their own business, but you can have ownership, however small, through buying the stock of a publicly traded company.

It's also fun to invest in something and watch it go up in value. There's a sense of pride in making a good decision. However, it's not as much fun when what you buy goes down in value. Learning about volatility is a valuable lesson we will also cover.

The Perfect Outfit

Building your investment portfolio is like putting together the perfect outfit. Stocks and bonds are like your top and bottom—they can be playful, feisty, or traditional (depending on your risk tolerance, the time horizon of the assets, and your financial goals). These two asset classes are often the primary drivers of your portfolio and typically make up the largest allocation (or portion).

Stocks have more opportunities for growth but also bring more volatility to the portfolio. A slinky low-cut number is more aggressive than a buttoned-up tailored shirt. Bonds tend to be more stable and provide the "cover your butt" portion of the portfolio (although not without risk). A sassy little skirt has less protection than a full-length pair of jeans.

Your accessories (shoes and jewelry) dress up the whole outfit and really make it come to life. Shoes are like your real estate properties; you might prefer a high rise (spiky heel) to a flat. Jewelry represents commodities, such as gold and silver. The correct amount of jewelry one puts on is in the eye of the beholder. It may or may not be necessary. You may like a lot of bling or be comfortable with none at all.

Your purse represents the cash in your portfolio. You might be hauling a large briefcase or something a little lighter.

What does your investment style look like? Do you like your outfit?

Sidenote: If you're not a fan of the outfit analogy, here is a similar analogy to food. If you prefer that option, you can view it this way:

- Protein (chicken, beef, tofu, lentils) = Stocks and equities
- Vegetables (broccoli, carrots, spinach) = Bonds and fixed income
- Beverage (milk, water, wine) = Cash and the money market
- Fruit (grapes, blueberries, apple) = Real estate
- Fat (olive oil, avocado, nuts) = Commodities

Asset Classes

These five pieces of your outfit align with the primary asset classes that are utilized in your portfolio. You may see portfolios that consist of all five asset classes or may just hold cash, stocks, and bonds. Real estate and commodities might be combined and called real property. There is no industry standard, which can be confusing. Stocks, bonds, and cash tend to be the most utilized asset classes and typically make up the largest component of a portfolio. Real estate, commodities, and other miscellaneous investments tend to make up a smaller portion or may not be appropriate for you.

Stocks = Ownership

Stocks, also called equity, are ownership in a company. If you own a hundred shares of 3M, you now own a portion of 3M. We typically buy stocks because we expect them to grow in value. If we paid $175 for each share of 3M, we are hoping it will go up in price, so we can sell it and make a profit (or a gain). Stocks move up and down in price, or have volatility. Stocks come in different shapes and sizes.

Stocks, also called equity, are ownership in a company.

Company Size Matters

There are large, medium, and small companies. You will hear them referred to as large-, mid-, and small-cap companies. Cap or capitalization is the size of the company. You take the number of outstanding shares times the current stock price to arrive at the capitalization. There are differing definitions of what size companies fall into large, mid, and small. I view large companies as $10 billion or more of market cap (Microsoft, Apple, Amazon, Facebook), mid as $2 to $10 billion (Crocs, Lending Tree, Skechers, Brinks), and small as less than $2 billion (Tupperware, GoPro, Barnes & Noble, Yeti).

Location, Location, Location

There are domestic (U.S.), developed-foreign (Europe, Australia, Far East), and emerging-foreign (China, Brazil, India, etc.) stocks. This categorization is determined by where the company is headquartered. Many domestic companies have a considerable portion of their revenue come from countries outside of the United States. I have had clients say they don't need any foreign investments because the companies they are invested in are doing business globally. There are really great companies headquartered outside of the United States that would be excluded if that approach is used. Some examples of non-U.S. companies you might recognize, include Nestle, Sony, Unilever (Ben & Jerry's, Vaseline, Hellman's, etc.), BMW, and Anheuser-Busch.

Growth Versus Value

Stocks can also be characterized as growth and value stocks. Growth stocks are considered to have the potential for price appreciation, tend to be more volatile, pay little or no dividends, and often use profits to reinvest back into the business. Value stocks are often mature companies with a lower possibility of price appreciation but reward shareholders with a higher payout of profits in the form of a dividend. They may also trade below what they are really worth, so it could be viewed as if you are buying the company on sale or getting it for a good "value."

Bond = Loan

Bonds, also called fixed income, are like loans. When you buy a bond, you have, in essence, loaned money to the underlying company, government, or municipality selling it. They are often considered a stable investment. However, the values do go up and down, and if you went to sell it prior to maturity, you could have a loss or a gain, depending on the current valuation. You can also lose everything if the company goes bankrupt or the project the bond is supporting fails. However, if there is anything to salvage from the company or project, the bondholder is higher in the credit structure, meaning they will receive money back before stockholders who are lower on the credit structure.

Bond also called fixed income, are like loans.

Fixed-Income Stream

Bonds often have a set interest rate (or yield). If you buy a bond for $10,000 and hold it for the term (length of time until maturity) of the bond, you will get back your $10,000. During the term, you will "clip the coupon" or receive the interest rate it pays. People often buy bonds for the fixed-income stream that the bond provides. Bonds are usually purchased to provide stability and income, not growth, in a portfolio.

Clipping Coupons

When bonds were first issued, the bond holder was physically given the bond, with coupons attached for each semiannual payment due to them during the term of the "loan." They were called bearer bonds. The holder (or bearer) of the bond could present the coupon for payment. My friend Lynn shared this story: "When I worked for the City of Des Moines in the 1980s, there was an older gentleman who would bring a briefcase full of City of Des Moines Bonds. We would clip the coupon off each bond, total up the interest payments, and then write out a check to him for that amount." The danger with bearer bonds was whoever presented the coupons would be paid. Of course, today bonds are issued electronically. No coupons to clip!

Bond Example

If you own a $10,000 bond yielding an interest rate of 2%, each year, you (the bond holder) will receive $200 of interest. If the term (maturity) of the bond is ten years, you will receive $2,000 during the length of ownership. At maturity, you will also receive back the initial $10,000 invested in the bond, unless there have been issues with the company or project as stated earlier.

Real Estate = Property

Real estate is investment property like office buildings, strip malls, apartments, warehouses, and data centers. There is often rent involved, which means a higher income stream is possible. Real estate can be volatile, which was never as apparent as during the 2008–2009 financial crisis, when the housing market crashed. Real estate is purchased for both income and growth.

Real estate is investment property like office buildings, strip malls, apartments, warehouses, and data centers.

REITs Versus Ownership

Real estate investment trusts (REITs) are the easiest way to get exposure to this asset class. They trade like a stock and provide diversification across multiple holdings. They can offer investments in different types of buildings and in different geographical locations. You could go out and buy one building, which is a much larger undertaking and is a concentrated (single) holding. Or, you could buy multiple buildings and now have some diversity and an income stream. Owning buildings also creates a liquidity issue. If you suddenly needed the money tied up in these buildings, it would likely take some time to sell the properties. You can't, within days, turn the building into cash. REITs typically are able to be sold and liquidated relatively quickly. You need to weigh the pros and cons of these different styles based on your situation.

Commodities = Gold

Commodities are bulk goods like gold, silver, energy (oil & gas), and agriculture. There is little that differentiates the gold one company is selling versus another. This can be a very volatile asset class. Commodities are typically purchased as a hedge against inflation. For example, if we go into an inflationary environment and it now costs you more to fill up the gas tank of your car, the value of your investment in crude oil should also go up in price. Having them in your portfolio can be a helpful way to offset (or hedge) against that type of environment.

Commodities are bulk goods like gold, silver, energy (oil & gas), and agriculture.

Miscellaneous

There are also other types of miscellaneous investments. Alternatives, such as hedge funds, venture capital or private equity as well as structured notes could also be investments in your portfolio. These are more complicated and beyond the scope of what we will cover in this book.

Volatility

Volatility is a given in investments; some asset classes experience more of it than others. The markets are going to go up or down, or could be relatively flat. What we've seen historically is the stock market generally goes up when viewed over long time periods. Think about it this way, when your favorite boutique—Ann Taylor, Athleta, LuluLemon—has a big sale, you're happy to get a great price. When the stock market goes down, view it as an opportunity to get your favorite company at a discount. Go bargain shopping!

INVESTMENTS
Simplified

RISK TOLERANCE	RISK/REWARD TRADEOFF	ASSET ALLOCATION
Ability & Willingness	Efficient Frontier	Diversification

Risk Tolerance

There is no "one size fits all" model when it comes to risk tolerance and no rule of thumb I'm comfortable suggesting. Your risk tolerance is unique to you. Applying the ability and willingness test is useful. The amount of money you have and the time horizon you're working with can help determine your ability to accept risk. However, if you aren't going to be able to sleep at night knowing how your assets are invested, then you don't have the willingness.

Your risk tolerance is unique to you.

Risk tolerance has a tendency to change based on how the stock market has behaved recently. If the market has been on an upward trend, we think we have a greater acceptance of risk. As soon as market volatility rears its ugly head, our risk tolerance is reduced. I observed this tendency during the dot.com bubble in 2000, in the financial crisis of 2008 and 2009, and most recently during the Covid-19 pandemic of 2020.

Tell me this, when you're in your car, do you drive the speed limit? Do you drive five to ten miles over the speed limit? Or, do you drive whatever speed you feel like driving? This could be another indicator of your approach to life—conservative, balanced, or aggressive, depending on which answer you selected.

Most of us don't really know how much risk we can tolerate until we experience a volatile market. Establish a long-term plan and try to keep the emotion out of current circumstance. During volatile markets, try to stay calm and steady; stick with your long-term plan. That will generally be the best approach. Making changes during a downturn or pullback in the market is typically the worst time to make that decision. History has shown over and over again that when the market rebounds, it does so quickly. It's impossible to time when that will happen. It's even harder to make the decision to get back in the market when you're sitting on the sidelines.

Risk-Reward Tradeoff

Portfolios can be structured to be conservative (more bonds than stocks), aggressive (more stocks than bonds) and everywhere in between. If you are willing to accept additional risk, you have the potential for higher returns over time. For example, if you put all your money into investment-grade bonds, you should have low risk but also expect a lower return. If you put all your money into stocks, you have greater risk but also a much higher opportunity for increased return.

If you are willing to accept additional
risk, you have the potential for
higher returns over time.

The efficient frontier plots a variety of portfolios on a graph with return moving up the vertical axis and risk moving across the horizontal axis. An efficient portfolio provides a return appropriate for the amount of corresponding risk taken. An inefficient portfolio is one that takes on more risk but doesn't receive the expected return.

You want your portfolio to land on the efficient frontier, but there is no right place to be on the efficient frontier. It's really dependent on your situation, your time horizon, your appetite for risk. Think back to your money values and the goals you want to achieve. This could help you determine the amount of risk you're willing to take and the return you want to achieve.

Asset Allocation

Asset Allocation is how you choose to invest Among the primary Asset classes we've been talking about (cash, stocks, bonds, real estate & commodities). Think about the perfect outfit. If possible, you want to have all pieces of the outfit. You shouldn't have all pants and no shirts or vice versa.

Diversification is going Down within each asset class. For example, within stocks, there are large, medium, and small companies and domestic (U.S.), developed-foreign (Europe, Australia, Far East), and emerging-foreign (China, Brazil, India, etc.) stocks. Splitting up assets among different investments within each asset class provides diversification. Refer to Asset Allocation and Diversification Table. Going back to the perfect outfit, you want to own more than one top. You might have sweaters, sweatshirts, button-down shirts, and long-sleeved tees. You want a variety to choose from when you're getting dressed in the morning. That is being diversified.

Asset Allocation and Diversification Table

Asset Allocation/Asset Class

	CASH	BONDS	STOCK	REAL ESTATE	COMMODITIES
Diversification	Money Market	Government	Domestic (US)	Real Estate Investment Trusts (REITs)	Gold/Silver
These are a few examples, but by no means an exhaustive list.	Certificates of Deposit (CDs)	Municipal	Developed Foreign	Office Buildings	Oil/Gas
	Treasury Bills	Corporate	Emerging Foreign	Strip Malls	Pork Bellies/ Live Cattle
	Commercial Paper	High Yield	Large, Mid, Small Cap	Apartments	Corn/Soybeans/ Wheat/ Coffee
		Treasury Inflation-Protected (TIPS)	Growth/Value	Industrial Buildings	

Asset allocation and diversification in your portfolio help smooth out what can be a bumpy market ride.

Asset allocation and diversification in your portfolio help smooth out what can be a bumpy market ride.

In 1986, researchers Gary Brinson, Randolph Hood, and Gilbert Beebower published "Determinants of Portfolio Performance" in the *Financial Analysts Journal* that demonstrated more than 90% of a portfolio's return is attributable to its mix of assets.[15] What does that mean? The decision regarding asset allocation or how much of your portfolio is invested in stocks versus bonds is the largest determinant to how your portfolio will perform.

Which individual stocks you choose, for example Coke or Pepsi, is less impactful.

---

[15] Gary P. Brinson, Randolph L. Hood, and Gilbert L. Beebower. "Determinants of Portfolio Performance, Financial Analysts Journal," vol.51, issue 1 (1995): 133-138, https://www.doi.org/10.2469/faj.v51.n1.1869.

INVESTMENTS
Simplified

INVESTMENT VEHICLES	INVESTING IN STOCKS	INVESTING IN FIXED INCOME
Individual (direct) Mutual Funds (active) Exchange Traded Funds — ETF's (passive)	Domestic Equity Developed Foreign Equity Emerging Foreign Equity Large, Mid, Small Cap Growth & Value	Government Bonds Municipal Bonds Corporate Bonds High Yield Bonds TIP's

Investment Vehicles

There are a variety of ways to create a portfolio. Some of the most commonly used investment vehicles are individual or direct purchase of the asset, mutual funds, and exchange-traded funds (ETFs).

Individual or direct purchase is when you (or someone on your behalf) is choosing the specific asset to be purchased within the asset class. For example, within stocks, it would be making the decision to purchase one stock over another. One of the most used examples is buying Coca Cola stock versus Pepsi stock—two competing companies in the same industry. Which will do better? Why would you buy one over the other? This takes a considerable investment in time and research to make a qualified decision.

> Some of the most commonly used investment vehicles are individual or direct purchase of the asset, mutual funds, and exchange-traded funds (ETF's).

Mutual funds provide a portfolio that is actively managed by a portfolio manager or team of portfolio managers. They are making active decisions to buy and sell stocks, bonds, or other underlying investment types. If we focus on a stock mutual fund, it will typically have a specific theme—like large companies with opportunity for growth or emerging-market companies headquartered in emerging-foreign countries like India, Russia, and Brazil.

The mutual fund is purchased with the anticipation that the portfolio managers will be able to outperform the appropriate index (or benchmark) over time. The reality is the mutual fund has the opportunity to both outperform or underperform. When investing in a mutual fund, you are hoping that the portfolio manager will be able to perform better than the market, so you are willing to pay for that possibility. There is a built-in expense ratio for every mutual fund. This is something you should know about any mutual fund in your portfolio.

ETFs are passively managed and mimic an index, like the Standard & Poor's 500 Index. There aren't any decisions being made other than to follow what the index is doing as closely as possible. When investing in an ETF, you are giving up the possibility of outperforming (or underperforming). You will get market returns. There is typically less cost associated with ETFs than mutual funds because you aren't paying people to do research and make decisions around what to buy, sell, and hold. The expense ratios for ETFs tend to be lower.

Note: there can be mutual funds that are passively managed and replicate an index, and there are ETFs that are actively managed. I am making broad generalizations about the two different vehicles.

Investing in Stocks

Stocks provide the opportunity for growth in your portfolio and also bring volatility. You can purchase individual stocks, mutual funds, or ETFs. We have talked about the different ways to get diversification within the stock asset class (refer to Asset Allocation and Diversification Table). You can purchase large, medium, and small companies and domestic (U.S.), developed-foreign (Europe, Australia, Far East), and emerging-foreign (China, Brazil, India, etc.) stocks. You can own a China fund that is focused on small-cap growth stocks. There are a variety of ways to get stock exposure in your portfolio.

Investing in Fixed Income

Bonds provide more stability and income, but they do have risk—some more than others. Bonds can appear on the surface to be relatively simple; however, they are a little more complicated than expected at first glance. One of the key concepts is that bond prices fall when interest rates rise and vice versa. This can be a difficult concept to wrap your head around.

There are a variety of bonds you can purchase—government, corporate, municipal, TIPS, or high yield.

- Government: Bonds issued by the government. Money is used for government spending. Income and capital gains may be taxable depending on the type of bond.
- Corporate: Bonds issued by a company. Money is used for operations, research, or acquisition of other companies. Income and capital gains are generally taxed at both the federal and state levels.
- Municipal: Bonds issued by state and local governments. These are federally tax-exempt and state tax-exempt if you purchase a bond from the state in which you reside (see example below). There are two types of municipal bonds:
  - General obligation bonds are not secured by any assets but by their power to tax residents.
  - Revenue bonds are backed by the revenue from a specific project or source.
- Treasury Inflation-Protected Securities (TIPS): Bonds that provide protection against inflation. They are backed by the government and adjust according to inflation. Income is subject to federal tax but not state and local taxes.
- High Yield: Bonds issued by companies that are considered to be at greater risk of not being able to return the principal amount you paid for the bond or pay the interest income due on the bond. Therefore, they pay a higher income (or yield). These are also referred to as non-investment-grade or junk bonds. They are treated like corporate bonds for tax purposes.

Each type of bond can have very different tax implications, as indicated in the descriptions. For example, you do not pay federal taxes on the income or yield (the $200 per year from the earlier bond example) received from municipal bonds (or munis as we call them). If you buy a muni bond issued in the same state in which you live, you will also not pay state taxes on the income. For example, I live in Minnesota, so if I buy a Minnesota muni bond, I will not pay federal or state taxes on the income. If I buy a California muni bond, I will not pay federal taxes, but I will pay state taxes. If you sell the bond at a gain, there will be taxes on the capital gain.

You can buy individual bonds and build what is called a bond ladder. A bond ladder has bonds maturing each year going out a length of time, such as fifteen years. Ideally, each year a bond matures and you have money available to use toward spending if so desired or needed. Otherwise, the decision can be made to reinvest in a bond that would mature beyond the longest bond on the ladder or invest in something else. It provides flexibility. There are also bond mutual funds and ETFs that can be purchased, as well as other individual bond strategies.

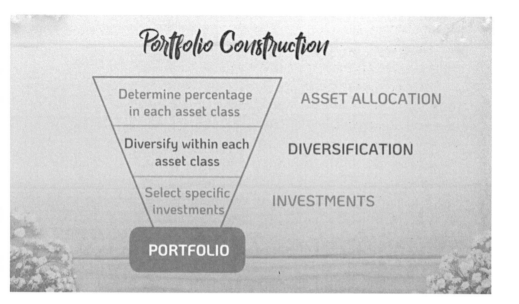

Portfolio Construction

Determine percentage in each asset class	ASSET ALLOCATION
Diversify within each asset class	DIVERSIFICATION
Select specific investments	INVESTMENTS

PORTFOLIO

Portfolio Construction

Typically, when creating a portfolio, you start with the higher-level decision of what percentage to have in each asset class. Then, you decide how to diversify within each asset class. Finally, you determine the specific investment. It's like a funnel working through the decision-making process and arriving at the final choice.

It's like a funnel working through the decision-making process and arriving at the final choice.

There are also investment vehicles that combine different investments, like stocks, bonds, and other asset classes. Retirement funds are a good example of this. You choose a fund that correlates with the year you are planning to retire. For example, if you turn sixty-five in 2030 and plan to retire that year, you could select a retirement fund that is designed for individuals retiring in 2030. The fund will then invest as they see appropriate for an individual retiring at that time. They will gradually reduce the exposure to stocks and other more volatile investments and increase the exposure to bonds and cash the closer it gets to the retirement date. The asset allocation decisions are made for you.

Take some time to review how your portfolio is currently allocated. How much do you have in the five primary asset classes: cash, stocks, bonds, real estate, and commodities? Think about the outfit. How is it diversified within each of those asset classes?

For example, within the stock asset class, what is the breakdown of the various equity categories (domestic, developed foreign, emerging foreign, small, mid, large)? Which investment vehicles are being used? Is it in individual stocks and bonds, mutual funds, ETFs, or a combination? What did you discover? Does it feel appropriate? Was it more aggressive or more conservative than you expected or thought? Is it invested so you can have a greater opportunity to achieve your goals?

Write your thoughts below:

_____

_____

_____

_____

_____

_____

_____

_____

_____

If there are holdings you don't understand in your portfolio, prepare a list of questions for your advisor. Learn more about those assets at your next meeting, or give your advisor a call today. Be proactive!

Write out a list of questions you want to ask here:
Write your thoughts below:

_____

_____

_____

_____

_____

_____

_____

_____

_____

Frequently Asked Questions (FAQs)

Frequently Asked Questions

Q: What's the difference between a financial advisor and a financial planner?

A: A financial advisor focuses primarily on the investment of your assets. A financial planner helps you lay out a plan for achieving your financial goals. There is often a lot of crossover between what they provide. An advisor may also offer planning, and a planner may also manage the investments. Typically, there is an element that they consider to be the most important aspect of their role, and that is where they will initiate conversations with prospective clients.

Ask them how they can provide the most value to your financial situation. What areas will they focus on with you? Ask them to explain how they differ from their competitors.

What you need from a financial professional could change over time. Understand what they offer and how they can grow with you.

Q: How do I find and hire an advisor?

A: Asking family and friends who they work with is a great starting point. If they like and trust the person or team they're working with, ask them to make an introduction.

The most important thing you can do is meet with at least three different providers. You are going to share all of your financial information with this individual. You want them to be a good personality fit with you. They should welcome your questions and be able to explain the answers in a way that you understand. This is your money, and you want to be involved in the discussion. If they aren't explaining it in a way that makes sense to you, that's on them, not on you.

In her book, *Lumination: Shining a Light on a Woman's Journey to Financial Wellness,* Heather Ettinger dedicates an entire appendix to questions to ask when looking for a financial advisor.[16] (She also includes a Financial Wellness Assessment for women of different ages that is really well done.) It's not impossible, but certainly not pleasant to terminate one advisor and move to someone else. It's also a fair amount of work, and there could be tax consequences and other issues. I would try to find the best possible match upfront.

If you don't have anyone to ask for a referral, looking for someone with the appropriate credentials would be the next step. A certified financial planner (CFP®) has taken classes and passed a rigorous exam. They are also held to certain ethical standards. You can look on the CFP board website https://www.cfp.net/ to find someone with this certification.

There are a number of other credentials that can be held. For example, a certified divorce financial analyst (CDFA) helps clients navigate the money issues involved in a divorce settlement, such as asset distribution, taxes, and financial planning. This might be a criteria for you to look for if you are going through a divorce, and you could benefit from this type of specialization.

Q: How are advisors compensated?

A: This is, unfortunately, a really difficult question. There are a variety of ways advisors and planners can be compensated, which makes it hard to make an apples-to-apples comparison of what each one will cost. Compensation typically occurs in one of three ways:

- Fee-only: The advisor charges specifically for the services they are providing. It can be an hourly rate, a fixed retainer for a specific

---

[16] Heather Ettinger. *Lumination: Shining a Light on a Woman's Journey to Financial Wellness*, (Hartford, CT: PYP Academy Press, 2020).

project or a defined period of time, or a percentage of the assets under management (AUM).

- Commission: The advisor earns money by selling certain products or services. The company whose product is being recommended could be paying them, or there could be a sales charge (load) that you are paying directly out of your pocket.
- Fee-based: This is a mix of fee-only and commission. They might charge a fee and earn a commission on specific products.

The most important thing when it comes to fees is understanding EXACTLY how the advisor is getting paid. Ask them to be very specific. Are they getting paid to make the best decisions for you or to make the most money for them?

One thing I do want to point out is the high level of fees associated with insurance and annuities. They can be appropriate in the right situation (we will talk about insurance and the importance in the next chapter), but I would definitely want to understand the compensation structure and benefit to the person selling it to you.

I remember meeting with a husband and wife who were prospects. When it came to the fee discussion, they told me their current advisor wasn't charging them anything. I assured them he was getting paid. He wasn't doing this out of the goodness of his heart; he likely had a mortgage to pay and a family to support. They just couldn't see what he was making. The fees or commissions were buried or hidden. It was not transparent. I encouraged them to go back and ask him to share with them how he was getting paid. They ended up hiring my team.

I personally have always worked on a fee-only basis. I do believe it reduces the conflict of interest that can be present in the other two approaches. I always wanted to be in the situation of being an advocate for the client and doing what was right for them, rather than being incentivized for any other reason.

Q: Do I need an advisor?

A: I think it's incredibly valuable to work with a professional in the financial area for a variety of reasons:

- They are working with other clients and have the opportunity to see many different situations. They can apply what they've experienced to your circumstances.

- An advisor has the ability to step back and make decisions with less emotion. That's hard to do when the money you're investing is your own. It's easy to get attached to your decisions and not want to make changes when you need to pivot. An outside set of eyes can bring a new perspective. A big part of my job was reassuring clients and trying to keep them from making bad decisions. It's easy to panic and do something that could significantly set you back, especially when markets take a sharp downturn.

- They are paying attention to what's happening in the world economically and politically and to the various markets on a daily basis. This is what they do every day, and they are likely thinking about the impact on various investment strategies far more than you ever will.

- Regardless of wealth level, they can help you think through ways to move forward in your situation that you may not have ever considered. They will have different strategies and ideas to recommend.

It is important to remember that this is YOUR money. I always felt it was my responsibility to provide my clients with the best advice possible. But if there was something that made them uncomfortable or that they strongly disagreed with, that was their prerogative. However, they could not then hold me accountable if something did not turn out the way they expected.

That's not to say advisors have all the right answers. They don't. There is no crystal ball. They don't know you as well you know you and your situation. That is why it is so important for you to learn as much as you can about the fundamentals so you can get involved in the discussion.

Q: So, it sounds like I should have an advisor. Who else do I need on my team?

A: I would recommend having an estate-planning attorney and an insurance specialist, which we are going to cover in more detail in the next chapter. There are often tax implications to be considered throughout your situation, so having a tax professional or certified public accountant (CPA) is also valuable.

As your wealth level increases, it is going to be important that these individuals are working together and talking to each other, so there is a complete understanding of your entire situation. You may also outgrow the professionals on your team. While loyalty is wonderful, you need to be confident that the team you've assembled is capable of handling a more complex financial situation.

Wrap Up Exercise: Pillar 5, Learn to Speak "Investments"

Take a moment and think about what surprises or "aha" moments you've experienced as a result of reading Pillar 5 and doing the exercises.

Write your thoughts below:

_____

_____

_____

_____

_____

_____

_____

_____

What would be one or two small steps you could take to move forward on your journey?

Write your thoughts below:

_____

_____

_____

_____

_____

_____

_____

_____

_____

Track Your Stock

Write down the price of the stock and the value of the DJIA and S&P 500:

Today's Date _____
DJIA _____
S&P 500 _____
Your Stock _____

How is your stock doing? Is it up or down from when you first wrote down the stock price?

Write your thoughts below:

_____

_____

_____

_____

_____

_____

_____

_____

_____

Consider these questions:

1. What news has been in the headlines recently?
    a. Political issues? Global issues? Environmental issues? Has the Federal Reserve been making any changes?
2. What has been happening with the overall market?
    a. Have the S&P 500 and DJIA been up or down?
    b. Has there been a lot of volatility or has it been relatively steady?
3. How has this been impacting your stock?
    a. Has it been up or down?
    b. Has it been tracking with the market or moving differently?
4. How do you feel about this?
    a. Comfortable, anxious, happy, sad?
    b. Has this provided any insights into your risk tolerance?

Write your thoughts below:

_____

_____

_____

_____

_____

_____

_____

_____

_____

Ellegant PILLAR 6

Protect and Plan

"Money is only a tool. It will take you wherever you wish, but it will not replace you as the driver."
—Ayn Rand, Russian-American writer and philosopher

Ellegant Pillar 6: Protect and Plan

Pillar 6 Key Concepts

1. Prepare myself (and my family) for the unexpected.
2. Be proactive around my entire financial situation, knowing that life happens.
3. Plan accordingly so I don't send my family on a scavenger hunt in the event of my untimely death.

Pillar 6 is all about wealth protection—insurance and estate planning. Insurance isn't much fun because you're paying for something that may never provide any benefit. Estate planning is all about your own death. Talk about good times. A rather heavy final pillar, yet incredibly important aspects of our financial situation.

This pillar takes all the work you've done in the previous five pillars and allows you to immortalize your values, goals, and wishes. It really does wrap it all up!

1 **What if something happened to you or your spouse/partner?**

What impact would that have on your financial well-being?

2 **Insurance protects what is important to you.**

It supplies peace of mind.

3 **Insurance provides financial leverage and control.**

This allows your estate to carry out your dreams.

Prepare for the Unexpected.

The best analogy I've heard with regard to insurance is a comparison to a toilet plunger. I adapted this from the book by Mitch Anthony, *The New Retirementality: Planning Your Life and Living Your Dreams...At Any Age You Want.*[17] You don't buy a plunger hoping to use it. You buy it in case your toilet backs up unexpectedly and then you're really happy you have one. Insurance is similar. You buy it in case something catastrophic happens—your house burns down or you or a family member are in a car accident.

Women have additional reasons for needing the appropriate insurance. We tend to live longer,[18] we outlive our husbands,[19] we have a higher

---

[17] Mitch Anthony. *The New Retirementality: Planning Your Life and Living Your Dreams...At Any Age You Want*, 4th ed. (Nashville, TN: John Wiley & Sons, 2014).

[18] Sherry Murphy, Jiaquan Xu, Kenneth Kochanek, and Elizabeth Arias. "Mortality in the United States, 2017." NCHS data brief no. 328 (November 2018). https://www.cdc.gov/nchs/products/databriefs/db328.htm.

[19] Sherry Murphy, Jiaquan Xu, Kenneth Kochanek, and Elizabeth Arias. "Mortality in the United States, 2017." NCHS data brief no. 328 (November 2018). https://www.cdc.gov/nchs/products/databriefs/db328.htm.

probability of spending time in a nursing home,[20] and we're at increased risk of dementia and Alzheimer's.[21] I know, not exactly uplifting news.

Insurance can also be an effective tool for transferring wealth to your loved ones. These are a little more complicated strategies that I would encourage you to discuss with your advisor if appropriate.

Take some time to review the insurance you currently have in place. As our stage of life changes, so do our insurance needs. There are some basics that we all require, such as health, auto (if you have a vehicle), and homeowner's or renter's insurance.

As our stage of life changes, so do our insurance needs.

There are other insurance and protections that you may need depending on your particular situation. Examples of other types of insurance coverage could be life, disability, umbrella liability, long-term health care, prescription drug or pet, to name a few.

Keep in mind that insurance is always evolving. One area in particular that has changed for the better, in my opinion, is long-term health care insurance. A few years ago, I wouldn't have considered looking into it for myself. It seemed expensive, and if you died and didn't need it, you lost it. Now, there are policies that provide a death benefit if you don't use the long-term care option. Sometimes, these things are worth a second look.

Having a conversation with your advisor or insurance specialist is going to provide some ideas around other potential insurance needs that make sense

---

[20] Richard Johnson. "What Is the Lifetime Risk of Needing and Receiving Long-Term Services and Supports?" Office of the Assistant Secretary for Planning and Evaluation (2019), https://aspe.hhs.gov/pdf-report/what-lifetime-risk-needing-and-receiving-long-term-services-and-supports

[21] Alzheimer's Association. "Women and Alzheimer's." (n.d.) Accessed December 15, 2020. https://www.alz.org/alzheimers-dementia/what-is-alzheimers/women-and-alzheimer-s#:~:text=Women%20at%20risk,-Alzheimer's%20disease%20is&text=Almost%20two%2Dthirds%20of%20Americans%20with%20Alzheimer's%20are%20women.,65%20is%201%20in%205.

for you. Be aware of people's biases. Some advisors who don't sell insurance could be less than enthusiastic about the idea. Some insurance specialists and advisors who do sell insurance could be inclined to think you need to be insured to the max. You may need to take the recommendations and arrive at a thoughtful decision that feels right to you.

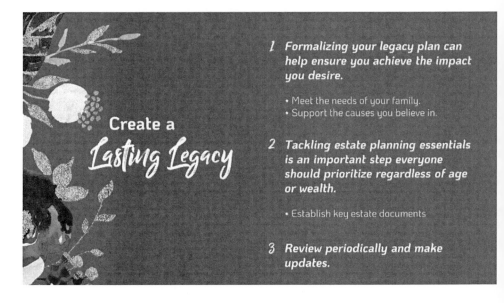

1 *Formalizing your legacy plan can help ensure you achieve the impact you desire.*

• Meet the needs of your family.
• Support the causes you believe in.

2 *Tackling estate planning essentials is an important step everyone should prioritize regardless of age or wealth.*

• Establish key estate documents

3 *Review periodically and make updates.*

Create a Lasting Legacy

Don't send your family on a scavenger hunt when you die. I've seen this happen all too often. Either the necessary planning hasn't taken place or nobody has been informed of the details. Your loved ones will be grieving; don't put this unnecessary stress on top of that. Take the time to get everything organized. Have a file that includes a listing of all of your accounts and passwords, along with important docu-

Don't send your family on a scavenger hunt when you die.

ments like your will, birth certificate, house title, etc. Then, talk to the people who need to know. Tell them your plans and wishes. Tell them where they can find the documents and information when the time comes. Be prepared.

I know this isn't a fun thing to think about. But providing a roadmap for your family will give you peace of mind knowing that your wishes will be carried out in the way you desire. It will also make things easier on your family when the time comes. Below are some of the documents to consider discussing with an estate planning attorney:

- Will
  - Provides what you want to have happen after your death. This covers property, funeral arrangements, children's guardians, and more.
- Durable Power of Attorney
  - Gives authority to someone else to make health care and financial decisions for you in a situation in which you can't make them for yourself.
- Advanced Healthcare Directive
  - Ensures healthcare decisions are carried out accordingly.
- Trusts (Living, Irrevocable)
  - Takes ownership of key assets, like your home, and prevents probate (public, costly, and lengthy legal process).

Have you done the appropriate estate planning for your life stage and wealth level? Or, do you have additional items to tackle?

Write your thoughts below:

_____

_____

_____

_____

_____

_____

_____

Your estate plan isn't a once and done document. It changes over time for a variety of reasons. Tax law changes can require updated thinking when it comes to your estate plan. Periods of transition, including getting remarried or divorced, losing a spouse, and your children getting married, are all times to revisit your documents. Plan to review your documents periodically.

If you have young children, please take the time to set up a will and select guardians for them, so it is clear who you want to care for them if something were to happen to you. Don't let the courts make that incredibly important decision for you.

My sister and brother-in-law were updating their documents when their children were fully grown with children of their own. In the previous document, my husband and I were named as the guardians for my niece and nephew, and we were naturally being removed. My niece, who at the time had three children of her own, jokingly said, "Wait a minute, you mean I don't get to live with Jayne and Nathan if something happens to you and Dad?"

Another really important component is to make sure all your beneficiaries are up to date. These items are referred to as direct designation forms because you specifically choose the beneficiary for that policy or plan. These direct designation forms override wills and other estate-planning documents. You want to check them at least annually and certainly after any type of significant event, like marriage, divorce, birth, or death of a family member. These include the following:

- Retirement plans, such as your 401(k), 403(b), IRAs (traditional, SIMPLE, SEP), and deferred-compensation employer plans
- Life insurance policies
- 529 education plans
- Bank or other accounts designated as "Transfer on Death"

One of the worst stories I heard was about a woman who got divorced, remarried, and had children with her new husband. But she didn't change the beneficiary designations that stated her ex-husband as the recipient. She died suddenly, and the ex-husband received her life insurance and 401(k). Don't make this mistake.

Another strategy to consider is 529 education plans. Setting aside money to be used for education for your children, grandchildren, niece, or nephew is a beautiful gift. A 529 education plan is an investment account for college savings that offers tax-deferred growth and other benefits.

My Heartfelt Legacy

Charitable giving tends to be important to women. We have an inherent need to give back. We care about the causes that have struck a chord in our hearts. This is an area you can be sure you've taken care of if your planning is in place.

Have you spent time thinking about the impact you want to make? Remember that your legacy is about what you do when you're living AND when you're gone.

Your legacy is also about so much more than money.

You can make a difference while alive by giving gifts now. This gives you the chance to watch the people you love enjoy the gift while you're still here. It also provides an opportunity to see how different people handle the gift. You might discover some are better stewards than others. This may change how you decide to distribute your assets after you're gone.

Your legacy is also about so much more than money. It goes back to your core values, to the money values and beliefs you're handing down. It's about how you treat people and the time you spend with them. It's the time, talents, and treasures you give to the people you love and the charities that are special to you.

Two of the questions I often hear women ask are, "Do I need to treat each of my children equally?" and "What if some of my children need more help than others?" This is a very personal decision. Nobody can give you that answer but you. I saw people who believed very strongly in the "equality is best" rule. Others, in particular those who had children with special needs or children who had followed a destructive path like drugs or illegal activity, didn't feel as compelled to follow that rule of thumb. Trusts can also be established with contingencies that need to be met before money can be paid out to the individuals. There are many options to consider on this front. This is a conversation you should have with your estate-planning attorney and advisor to determine the best plan of action.

Take some time to ponder what feels right and what you want that to look like—both now and after you're gone.

Write your thoughts below:

_____

_____

_____

_____

_____

_____

_____

Wrap Up Exercise: Pillar 6, Protect and Plan

Take a moment and think about what surprises or "aha" moments you've experienced as a result of reading Pillar 6 and doing the exercises.

Write your thoughts below:

_____

_____

_____

_____

_____

_____

_____

_____

What would be one or two small steps you could take to move forward on your journey?

Write your thoughts below:

_____

_____

_____

_____

_____

_____

_____

_____

_____

Track Your Stock

Write down the price of the stock and the value of the DJIA and S&P 500:

Today's Date _____
      DJIA _____
      S&P 500 _____
      Your Stock _____

How is your stock doing? Is it up or down from when you first wrote down the stock price?

Write your thoughts below:

_____

_____

_____

_____

_____

_____

_____

_____

_____

Consider these questions:

1. What news has been in the headlines recently?
   a. Political issues? Global issues? Environmental issues? Has the Federal Reserve been making any changes?
2. What has been happening with the overall market?
   a. Have the S&P 500 and DJIA been up or down?
   b. Has there been a lot of volatility or has it been relatively steady?
3. How has this been impacting your stock?
   a. Has it been up or down?
   b. Has it been tracking with the market or moving differently?
4. How do you feel about this?
   a. Comfortable, anxious, happy, sad?
   b. Has this provided any insights into your risk tolerance?

Write your thoughts below:

_____

_____

_____

_____

_____

_____

_____

_____

_____

"I can't change the direction of the wind, but I can adjust my sails to always reach my destination."
—Jimmy Dean, Country Music Singer

Ellegant Wrap-Up
Now what?

Your journey with money requires your commitment for a lifetime.

You've taken the time to invest in yourself. Hopefully, you've had some amazing insights and learned some new lingo.

But it doesn't end here. Your journey with money requires your commitment for a lifetime, not however long it took you to read this book. As you experience life events (and you will), your financial, investment, and estate-planning needs will change as well.

 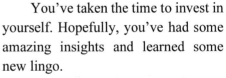

Unfortunately, this isn't a "wash, rinse, and repeat" kind of thing. There will be new challenges every time there's a shift in your life. I view that as positive, providing you with new learning opportunities.

I know, unfortunately, that some of these life events will not be pleasant or happy occasions. But I also know that you have placed yourself in a much stronger position of handling these events than before by actively pursuing an increased knowledge base.

ELLEGANT
WEALTH

SIX PILLARS TO FINANCIAL EMPOWERMENT

1	2	3
EXPLORE YOUR MONEY BELIEFS	**ESTABLISH YOUR FINANCIAL GOALS**	**KNOW YOUR NET WORTH**
"Marry a Rich Man"	What's Your Destination?	Financial Starting Point

4	5	6
SPEND WITH PURPOSE	**LEARN TO SPEAK "INVESTMENTS"**	**PROTECT AND PLAN**
Treasures, Promises & Joy	The Perfect Outfit	Giving the Best Gifts

You have successfully completed the Six Pillars to Financial Empowerment. Each pillar builds on the other. Combined, they will provide you with a comprehensive view of your financial situation.

What was the most significant surprise, inspiration, or "aha" moment you had for each pillar? As you look back at each pillar, where you wrote down one or two things you could work on, what really stood out? What really tugs at your heart?

I would love to see you make one or two promises, or commitments, to yourself. Write them down. Give yourself a deadline.

Is there someone you could have as an accountability partner? Someone who will hold you to the task you've selected?

Write your thoughts below:

_____

_____

_____

_____

_____

_____

_____

_____

_____

Is the commitment you made one that you wrote down originally after completing the pillar? Or, did you discover something new as a result of having completed all the pillars?

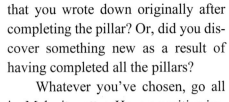

Whatever you've chosen, go all in. Make it matter. Have a positive impact on your financial life and possibly (probably) your family and your community.

Whatever you've chosen, go all in.

Complete the financial wellness quiz again. Circle which personality represents you now: blissfully unaware, definitely distressed, casually curious, or financially focused. Look back at where you were when you began this journey.

Did you move up a notch or two? Are you feeling more confident as you answer the questions? Think back to the first time you took it and where you were in your financial journey at that starting point.

If you've been reading and taking the time to think about the questions being asked, you should be feeling better about what you know. Sometimes, when we learn more, we realize how little we know. Don't let that discourage you. I've been working in this business for a long time and still don't have all the answers. There will always be more to learn. But you've taken huge steps forward.

Write your thoughts below:

_____

_____

_____

_____

_____

_____

_____

_____

_____

ELLEGANT
WEALTH

Celebration!

Congratulations! Thank you for your hard work and dedication. It has been my honor to be your guide.

By fully engaging in this book, you have already made meaningful strides in your financial journey. Your financial confidence has been inspired, and you are empowered to take on the world with courage, confidence, and wisdom.

Now, take the time to CELEBRATE!

About the Author

After thirty-four years of managing wealth for high-net-worth individuals and wealthy families across the United States, Jayne made the leap to entrepreneurship. She is uniquely qualified, with REAL experience and a variety of certifications and credentials. But even more important, she has an intense passion for providing women with a way to learn about money that's enjoyable and fun—yes, fun!

Jayne worked for large corporations such as U.S. Bank, Piper Jaffray, and Cargill/Waycrosse. She has her master's in business administration (MBA) from the University of St. Thomas, was a certified financial planner, is a certified career coach & counselor from Adler Graduate School, and is a results-based trained coach through the NeuroLeadership Institute.

Jayne observed first-hand the overwhelming feelings that divorced or widowed women experienced when they had not been engaged (or in some cases not even included) in the conversations about their financial situations. She decided to step away from managing investments to focus on closing the financial education gap by teaching women to demand what they need and deserve. Jayne transforms women from "deer in headlights" to financial superstars!

A "nice" Minnesotan who grew up in International Falls, the icebox of the nation on the Canadian border, Jayne grew up with ten sets of aunts and uncles and forty-seven cousins. She learned how to drive a stick-shift in Duluth in the middle of winter (she doesn't recommend it), loves lake-related activities in both summer and winter, and is no stranger to the long Minnesota goodbye. Her son and brother were Minnesota State hockey champions forty years apart, and she's been married to her best friend for almost thirty years.

Acknowledgements

To my husband, Nathan, for believing in me, especially at times when I didn't believe in myself. I couldn't have pushed through this past year without you.

To my dad for showing me money is fun and good. To my mom for teaching me to be responsible with money. To both of them for demonstrating a strong work ethic and for their encouragement and support.

To my son, Tyler, you will always be the center of my world and most cherished accomplishment. I am so proud of you and am constantly amazed at your intellect and passion. To my daughter-in-law, Stephanie, for the joy you bring to all of us. We are blessed to have you in our family. To my grand-dog, Oakley, for unexpectedly lighting up my life.

To the amazing coaches and instructors I have had on this entrepreneurial journey, Paula Winkler, Jasna Burza, Mark LeBlanc, Dr. Jermaine M. Davis, Robin Kellogg, Mike Gregory, and Deirdre Van Nest, for their wisdom and occasional push.

To my unofficial advisory board, Paula Carlson, Kate Lyons, Heidi Humphrey, Jacie Fogelberg, Lynn Maaske, Geetu Sharma, Paula Melo Doroff, Cat Breet, Jasmine Stringer, and Amy Vasterling—you are the amazing women I turn to when I need help thinking through an issue, a shoulder to cry on, or a celebratory glass of wine.

To my incredible marketing team, Lori Knisely, Sarah Cords, and Spencer Knisely for perfectly bringing my brand to life in a way I never could have imagined.

To Angela Divine Knox for beautifully creating my social media presence.

To Chis Jenkins for the many hours of guidance and mentoring.

To former clients (and friends), Dave & Jean Dovenberg, Nancy JP Anderson, and Amy Andersen for believing so much in me you had family and friends participate in my program.

To Maureen Aitken and Ann Aubitz for making this book even better.

There are so many others I want to acknowledge who have helped me on this journey. If I have not named you specifically, please know that I appreciate all that you have done for me.

Signature Offerings

You've read the book and now you want more? Jayne offers a variety of exciting ways for you to take the next step in your financial journey. Check out the Signature Offerings at www.ellegantwealth.com and discover:

- In-person group coaching sessions
- Six-week challenges
- Do-it-yourself online course
- One-on-one sessions

Choose the opportunity that works best for you! If you're not sure of the right next step, reach out to Jayne or sign up for a Discovery Chat at www.ellegantwealth.com.

> *"There is something I love about how the whole experience demystifies financial jargon and explains the essential concepts in simple actionable ways."*
> – Course Participant

ELLEGANT WEALTH
Inspiring Financial Confidence

Speaking Engagements

Jayne is an inspiring and engaging speaker. Any or all of the Six Pillars to Financial Empowerment make great topics for presentations to the groups, associations, and organizations to which you belong.

Share this impactful message with your friends. Reach out to hire Jayne as your next speaker at www.ellegantwealth.com.

"Never in a million years could I have imagined how powerful this workshop would be!"
– Workshop Participant

Connect with Jayne
Email: jayne@ellegantwealth.com
Website: https://www.ellegantwealth.com
Facebook: https://www.facebook.com/EllegantWealth
LinkedIn: https://www.linkedin.com/in/jayne-ellegard/
Instagram: https://www.instagram.com/jayne_ellegard/

A Special Gift

Financial Empowerment for Women: Your Guide to Courage, Confidence & Wisdom! is a wonderful gift to share with other women. Make a difference in someone else's financial life! Pass your book onto a friend or, even better buy them their very own copy.

Special discounts are available on quantity purchases by advisors/planners, attorneys, and accountants who would like to send a copy of this book to each of their female clients.

Discounts are also offered to corporations and associations who recognize the benefit this book would provide to their employees or members.

For details, contact Jayne at jayne@ellegantwealth.com.

ELLEGANT WEALTH

Inspiring Financial Confidence